KNIVES

KNIVES

An illustrated encyclopedia of
knives for fighting, hunting, and survival

PAT FAREY

THE LYONS PRESS

A SALAMANDER BOOK

Published in the United States by
The Lyons Press
Guilford, CT 06437.
www.lyonspress.com
The Lyons Press is an imprint of The Globe Pequot Press.

© Salamander Books Ltd., 2003

A member of **Chrysalis** Books plc

ISBN 1-59228-108-7

1 2 3 4 5 6 7 8 9 10

CREDITS
Project Manager: Ray Bonds
Designer: Cara Hamilton
Line drawings: JB Illustrations
Reproduction: Anorax Imaging Ltd
Printed and bound in China

THE AUTHOR

Pat Farey is the editor of *GunMart* and is a regular contributor to *Shooting
Sports* magazine. Apart from writing modern hunting and utility knife
reviews in both magazines, he also reports every month on the sale of
antique, ethnic and collectible edged weapons from Bonhams, Christie's,
Sothebys, Wallis and Wallis, and other auction houses.

ACKNOWLEDGMENTS
The publishers thank the individuals and firms who have contributed photographs
or loaned knives for photography so that they may be reproduced in this book: Pat
Farey, J and C Gower, Colin Pearce, Pete Moore, Bruce Potts (Sylvan Films), Alan
Wood, Geoff Hague, Graham Holbrook, Mick Wardell, Attleborough Accessories,
Bonhams, Crosscut (UK) Ltd., Framar, Heinnie Haynes, Whitby & Co., J. Adams
Ltd., British Museum, Columbia River Knife & Tool, KA-BAR Knives Inc., Gerber
(Fiskars Inc.), Camillus Cutlery Co., SOG Specialty Knives Inc., A. Eikhorn GmbH
& Co. KG, George Ibberson (Sheffield) Ltd., Benchmade Knife Company Inc.,
Kershaw Knives (KAI USA Ltd.), Outdoor Edge Cutlery Corp., Buck Knives,
Egginton Group (Sheffield), Heinr. Böker Baumwerk GmbH, United Cutlery Corp.,
Conaz Coltellerie dei Flli Consigli & C. s.n.c., EKA-knivar AB, Leatherman Tool
Group, Inc., Ontario Knife Co., Victorinox, Wenger, Cold Steel Inc., David Watson,
Farid www.faridknives.com

Contents

Introduction

NO MATTER how your time is spent, how you earn your living or what sports or hobbies you participate in, it's almost certain that at some point in the day you will have to use a knife. It may be buttering a piece of toast at home, sharpening a pencil in the workshop, cutting through ropes or other materials in the field, pruning plants in the garden, opening a letter at the office, cleaning a fish by a river, cutting up cardboard boxes at a store... the list is endless. Even in this high tech world a knife is still one of man's most important tools, and, as proved in the events leading up to the terrorist destruction of the World Trade Center, it can still be used as a deadly weapon.

In this book I hope to show how knives have developed over the years, from the earliest of man's tools right up to the present day, how some materials and designs have changed, while others have stayed basically the same. Why different interpretations of the same basic layout – a blade with a handle – have developed around the world to the extent that a book of ten times this size could not hope to cover all the various permutations of this very simple format.

There are many specialist knives for various trades and professions, from chefs to surgeons, but they are mostly beyond the scope of this book. So, although some specific trade knives are included, most of the models that are covered with here fall into the general category of personal tools. These include penknives, folding knives of various types, multi-tools, fixed-blade hunting and utility knives, military, survival and rescue knives, in fact any knife that might be used

Right: A knife for the 21st century? This is the new "Superknife" from the USA, a hybrid design that combines the convenient properties of folding pocket knives and removable blade craft knives

Left (top to bottom): George Wostenholme "IXL" penknife with jigged bone handles and silver inlay (circa 1930), Sheffield-made Rodgers horn handled knife with clip point blade, traditional pattern laguiole style French lock blade knife, made by G.David.

for field sports, other outdoor recreations, and hobbies, and by the armed forces. With the exception of the military knives, in the main these are the types that are regularly carried by ordinary citizens, and as such they are as much personal possessions as they are tools.

FORM AND FUNCTION

I remember as a child being fascinated by the local boot-mender (cobbler) and knife sharpener who had a shop at the end of the road where I lived. My fascination was partly due to the fact that part of the shop was given over to hardware supplies, particularly knives and edged tools. But my main interest was in watching the boot-mender at work, either when he was sharpening blades on his belt-driven circular stone, manually powered via a foot treadle, or when he was repairing shoes and boots on his last. He would cut and trim through layers of thick, heavy leather at lightening speed, his knife slicing through the tough material with apparent ease. The flexible "snobs" knife he used was named after another term for his trade,

and I was spellbound by his skilled use of it. Yet this wasn't some expensive professional tool. It was home-made, the blade being shaped from a piece of scrap steel (from the wide broken blade of an industrial machine "arm" saw). The grip was formed from a short length of wooden broom handle, split into two scales then secured to the blade's "tang" with insulating tape and whipped over with ordinary parcel string.

The boot-mender had shaped the blade on his grinding wheel and had hand-filed a small stitch-cutting "pick" on the end of it, so it looked much like a modern "guthook" knife. When the blade became too narrow through constant sharpening, or if it broke (it

Below (left to right): "Gillwell" Boy Scout sheath knife with matching skinning knife c1930s, commemorating Gillwell Park, the first Boy Scout campsite, made by Wade & Butcher, Sheffield, England. A 20thC sheath knife with stacked leather grip by Wade & Butcher. Another 20thC Wade & Butcher sheath knife, with antler handle. An antler handled 20thC sheath knife by George Wostenholme, Sheffield, England.

was quite a brittle steel if flexed too far), he simply made another one. He went to all this trouble, yet in his hardware shop he was surrounded by professionally made cutlery from tiny penknives through to billhooks and scythes, with every kind of camping, craft and kitchen knife in between.

The point is, that his home-made knife did the job, and probably did it as well as any professionally constructed blade. It fulfilled the first requirement of any such design – it was functional. In truth, this is all that we should expect from a working knife.

However, nobody could have said that the boot-mender's knife was good-looking, and this brings us to a second important requirement that we might also consider, usually described as "form." This refers to how something looks or how it feels, the visual and the tactile elements of the design. As any first year design student will tell you, if your product has "form and function" in the right blend, then you are on to a winner.

The same rules can be applied to any man-made objects, but in knives we see far greater consideration given to form. For instance, you might get a dozen knives all based on the very functional "bowie" knife, yet they might all be different in weight and size, they may have subtly different accents on the blade shape, the handle contours and materials, the cross guard and pommel, and so on. In addition, there might be inlays, etching or engraving, or various other types of decoration. In short, you could have a dozen totally different knives, yet they would all be classed as "bowies."

Above: Style can be expressed very differently even in knives of the same type, as seen in these three bowie knives; (left to right) a modern "Outlaw" survival knife, a traditionally designed bowie by Middleton Bros of Sheffield, and "The Highlander", a radical but functional version of the bowie by free thinking knife designer, Gil Hibben.

Left: Collectable barrel knife with 6" blade by "Joh Engstrom, Eskilstuna, Sweden 1784"; the folded blade was pulled from the handle, opened, then re-inserted into the wooden "barrel" handle to form a fixed blade knife.

Below: Rare Italian Rondel dagger with bone handle and pierced gothic decoration, circa 1450.

There is no absolutely correct "form" in knives – beauty is most definitely in the eye of the beholder – and it's the infinite variations created by individual designers that separate knives from other tools. When you set out to buy a screwdriver or a hammer you are almost certainly just looking for function. If it's the type of screwdriver or hammer that you need for your particular task, then that will usually do. Rarely would you be looking for any esthetic appeal. With knives for personal use it is different. You may well look for a knife that will do the job that you require of it, but you will almost certainly give some consideration to what it looks like and how it feels in the hand. When selecting a personal knife most people will give equal consideration to form and function when making their choice – and they may not even realise that they are doing it.

COLLECTING KNIVES

It is because of this important element of form that we have such a vast choice of knives available to us. In extreme instances the "form" part of the equation becomes more important than the "function," and I've known a few people who treat their knives almost like jewelry or as accessories that "say something" about the carriers (or wearers?). They will demonstrate the fine quality and workmanship of their prized possessions, and may even invite you to test the blades' edges…. But ask some of them to perform a useful task with their knives and they'll look at you aghast! These people enjoy ownership of their knives for their form alone, and who can blame them, because some of today's knives, especially those by custom blade-smiths, really do approach the description *objets d'art.*

At the extremes of form are the "fantasy" knives, some of which offer absolutely no pretensions regarding functionality of design, having no real use at all apart from being excellent collectors' pieces.

At one time collectors were interested only in antique or historic knives, but now there are so many well made and fine looking modern designs available that a whole new market has opened up among collectors. Some may collect one type of knife, or knives from one

Right: Custom hunting dirk, made by Alan Wood, with a blade made of "Odin's Eye" pattern Damascus steel, with a whale tooth handle and bronze fittings.

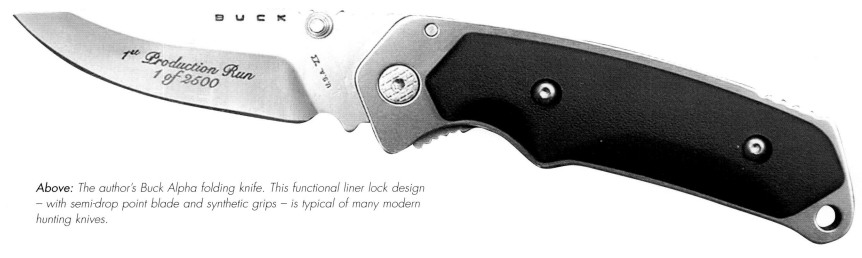

Above: The author's Buck Alpha folding knife. This functional liner lock design – with semi-drop point blade and synthetic grips – is typical of many modern hunting knives.

particular manufacturer, or possibly the work of just one designer. Others prefer to establish a more widely representative collection.

Hopefully, budding collectors will find this book useful in establishing exactly in which direction they wish to specialise – historic, ethnic, period, type, make, modern or simply general. They will certainly find a number of different avenues to explore and a good grounding in the basics of knife construction.

Right: One of the author's favourite working tools – a 1950s pattern British Army issue jack-knife, but still available today.

WHICH KNIFE?

For those who put function before form, and I personally err to this side of the equation, within this book you should find examples of most types of knives that are available from various parts the world today. It would be impossible to be completely comprehensive, or even representative of every type, make and designer, but I have tried to cover all the most important styles and models.

If you know the main tasks that your knife will be required to handle, then you should be able to choose the best model for the task. You will find sections on most of the blade and handle materials, fittings, lock types, folding and fixed designs, blade patterns, and so on – more than enough information to enable you to make an informed choice when deciding what kind of knife will be right for you. There's also a section on blade sharpening and maintenance, so once you have purchased your knife you will be able to keep it in optimum condition.

As for my own choices, of all the knives I have ever owned, I've felt most at home with an old army issue jack-knife (lost in action!), a Western Cutlery drop point folder (now in genteel retirement) and, at present, a Ken Onion designed folder by Kershaw (love at first sight) and a Cold Steel "Land & Sea, Rescue" (tough enough). You may have noticed that they are all folders, but that type of knife suits the work I put it to. There have been several fixed blade knives that I've been fond of, but I just don't get much chance to use them nowadays. One of my favorites, a hunting bowie, also made by Western Cutlery about twenty years ago, was given to my best friend, simply because it wasn't getting much use with me, and he needed a good skinner. I now have a modern Buck Alpha Hunter that makes occasional trips into the field with me, and it not only looks good, but it also does the business – form and function again.

For twenty years I worked as a steel erector, and a good working knife was an absolute necessity. Yet even though I had some excellent professionally produced knives available to me, I regularly made knives of a similar sort to that I'd seen the boot-mender make when I was a child, except mine had a sheep's foot style blade. The reason that I made these ugly but functional blades was that I had become fed up with dropping and losing expensive knives, or having them

Right: This is one of the many patterns of Swiss Army knife that have become famous world-wide as general purpose pocket tools. This particular model is the Victorinox Classic, designed specifically for the civilian market and suitable for men or women.

permanently "borrowed" by friends and colleagues who obviously found the "form" of my shop-bought rigging knives as attractive as I had when I purchased them. So instead I used my home-made working knives for years, along with a mini sharpening steel that doubled as a marlin spike. The home-made knives might not have been attractive, but they were functional and they were also free.

However, I would be the first to admit that I never became attached to my home-made work knives in the same way that I did to my old Western Cutlery drop point folder. Perhaps it was because of their lack of form. They weren't the "complete" package, whereas the Western Cutlery knife most definitely was.

SERVICE BLADES

Although this book mainly addresses knives used for sports and hobbies, and those sought after by collectors, a substantial part deals with knives used as tools and weapons by military and other services. After all, as well as being the world's most widespread tool, on occasion the knife will also double as the most basic and personal of man's weapons. Here I have looked at some fascinating and some downright plain and utilitarian bayonets, general issue combat/utility knives, specialist fighting knives, survival knives and rescue tools. Sometimes there's a cross-over between the civilian and military markets, with each sector influencing the other; for instance, the KA-BAR and the Swiss Army knives are perfect examples of designs that have proved popular in both fields. Once again, while the whole subject is too vast to be tackled comprehensively here, the coverage should give a general overview on military design trends.

LAST BUT NOT LEAST

When reading this book you may well find that some of the opinions expressed do not quite mesh with what you have read or been told before. This is probably because I don't make, sell or endorse knives, and what I have written comes solely from the viewpoint of a user and reviewer without vested interest. Some of the knives illustrated throughout the book will show signs of wear and tear – many of these are mine, or belong to colleagues and friends who give their knives hard use everyday in their occupations or hobbies. Others shown here may be new and unused, direct from the manufacturer, or they are collectors' pieces.

Finally, I would ask that if you ever borrow a knife from a friend, make sure that you give it back, otherwise you may end up losing a good friend, but even worse, he may end up losing a good knife....

Pat Farey, 2003

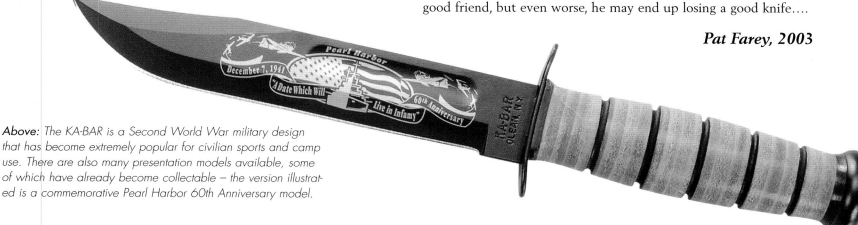

Above: The KA-BAR is a Second World War military design that has become extremely popular for civilian sports and camp use. There are also many presentation models available, some of which have already become collectable – the version illustrated is a commemorative Pearl Harbor 60th Anniversary model.

The Origins of Knives

THE FIRST sharp tool that our Stone Age ancestors used was probably a fractured rock (likely a flint) or a shell with a naturally sharp edge, used for cutting, skinning, scraping or as a weapon for hunting or fighting. It would have been picked up from the ground and used exactly as it was found. Samples of these edged tools dating as far back as 2,500,000 years have been found in Africa. They would have been vital to the everyday survival of the small groups of hunter-gathers that lived in these prehistoric days, since they were the only carnivores that were not equipped with sharp teeth and claws. Instead they had a large brain and an opposable thumb – they had to learn how to make tools and how to use them.

It was only a matter of time before naturally found stone tools were being improved by man and shaped into utensils for specific purposes. This was done by knapping – which means tapping off fairly large pieces of flint to get a basic shape – then using a finishing process called "pressure flaking" for the final edge. This technique required considerable skill and was achieved by applying pressure to the flint with a piece of hard wood or antler, causing flakes or slivers of stone to be removed until a fine sharp edge was produced. These first stone "knives" had no handles, but would simply be held directly in the hand. Later the grip portion of the tool was wrapped with animal skin or grass for a better hold, or a hide or leaf pad could be held in the palm of the user's hand with the knife cupped in it.

When the idea of fitting a haft or handle came about, the first knife in this form would have been a flint completely set into a split wooden haft, with the sharpened edge protruding from it. The hafted cutting edge gave the user better control and greater power in cutting and scraping. Eventually a tool evolved with the blade attached to the end of the haft – taking on the shape of the modern knife – and giving the implement an added use... it could now be employed for piercing or stabbing. Although most knives were fashioned from stone, especially flint, other materials were used, including a type of volcanic glass called obsidian, shells, animal bones, teeth, horn and even wood.

REFINEMENTS

Examples of Neolithic (New Stone Age) period tools have been found with some of the roughness of the flint removed by polishing to give a finer, cleaner edge, capable of deeper cuts. These smoother edges were made by rubbing the tool with or against an abrasive stone, and this method is still used today by the aborigines of Australia, New Guinea and some remote areas of South America. Ancient Egyptians chipped flints to give them a serrated edge, and then fitted handles to them by gluing them into wooden hafts and then binding them. The third to sixth millenniums BC were probably the epoch of stone knifemaking, with some Near and Middle Eastern ceremonial flint daggers being superbly formed and fitted

Left: Obsidian is a glassy volcanic rock, and has been used (along with flint and chert) by some cultures to make knives from the Stone Age right up until fairly modern times. This obsidian bladed knife is circa 1880 from the Admiralty Islands in the South Seas, and examples of "stone-age" knives are still used by some remote native tribes.

with decorated handles made of ivory, bone or horn.

Although the use of stone for knives was limited because of its brittleness and inflexibility, the positive qualities should not be underestimated. Care and skill were needed in the use of a stone knife, but ancient man had these skills and he knew the frailties of the material. Having seen video footage of a New Guinea tribal hunter skinning a monkey with a hand-held stone blade – little more than a sliver of flint – I would say that a modern hunter with a steel knife couldn't have made a better or quicker job of it.

Nevertheless, because of the fragile nature of the material, in general stone knives were usually fairly short and simply designed – it was not until the arrival of metal blades that knives could be made longer and with more complex shapes.

COPPER

Of the metal ores that primitive man could readily find as usable nuggets on the earth's surface, only copper lent itself to practical knifemaking. Gold and silver were also used, but they were softer and used more in decorative or ceremonial knives. There was also the chance of encountering meteoric iron – lumps of iron found in meteorites. This was a better material for knifemaking and could be hammer-formed, but it was extremely rare.

Copper nuggets were soft enough to be cold-formed by hammering, and this pounding process also compacted the metal, making the edge harder and suitable for use in cutting. Hammering also made the metal brittle, but this problem could be solved by an annealing process – heating and then quenching in water.

The next advance was in the discovery that nuggets of copper could be melted and cast. This meant that the size of the tool was no longer limited to the size of a single nugget, since two or more nuggets could now be combined by melting. Blades were usually

Below: A flint blade made by Native Americans indians approximately 9,000BC on the east side of the Rocky Mountains. This style flint knife is described as Folsom (after the place in New Mexico where the type was initially discovered) – it is characterized by a shaped edge all around, a fairly broad point and a concave base.

Above: A modern reproduction of a bone handled, shaped obsidian blade knife with leather and bead decoration in the style of Native Americans.

cast flat with a simple spike tang for the attachment of a handle.

About a thousand years after man started to use copper, the process of smelting (as opposed to melting) was discovered. By heating rock containing copper ore (such as malachite) to 700-800 degrees Centigrade, with the ore in direct contact with charcoal, droplets of copper could be sweated out, and then recovered when the fire was extinguished. This must have been a difficult process for early man since an ordinary "open" wood fire will reach a temperature of only around 600deg C, so a forced draught had to be introduced to achieve the extra 100-200deg C needed for smelting. This was a massive step forward in technology, and variations on the smelting process are still used to recover many metals from ore to this very day.

THE BRONZE AND IRON AGES

Around 3,000 BC the smelting process led to the discovery of bronze, an alloy of copper and tin bearing ores. The tin content allowed the metal to be produced in a fluid state at a lower temperature than copper alone, and it could be cast more easily in a split mold.

The ancient Greeks forged bronze knives and were also responsible for the development of metal rivets for attaching handles (usually of organic material) – another great step forward in knifemaking technology. Bronze was a much harder and stronger metal than un-alloyed copper, and therefore capable of being forged into larger edged weapons (such as swords). Forged bronze blades have been found in several countries, but some of the finest have unsurprisingly come from the ancient civilisations of the Near and Middle East.

Iron is one of the most abundant metals on the planet, and once it became possible to separate it from rock it became a popular

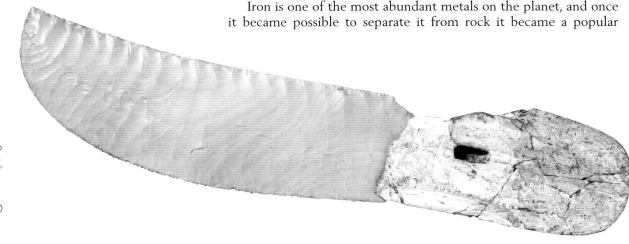

Right: The "Pitt-Rivers knife" – a flint bladed knife mounted in a decorated ivory handle from Sheikh Hamada, Egypt, made around 3,100 BC. The flint has been finely pressure flaked on one side only, removing small slivers to give a pattern termed as 'ripple-flaked', and the use of decorated ivory rather than wood suggests that it is likely this knife was purely ceremonial. (Photo: © British Museum)

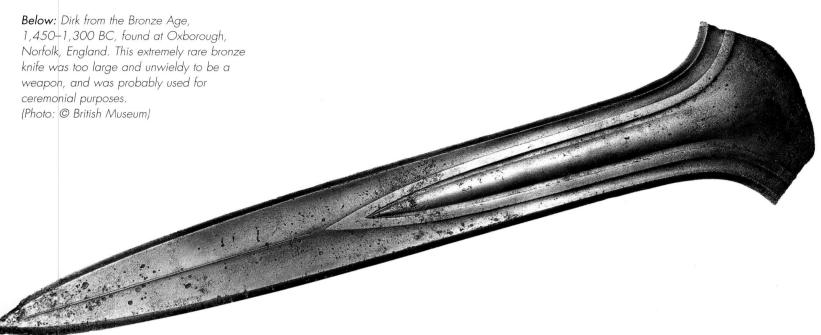

Below: Dirk from the Bronze Age, 1,450–1,300 BC, found at Oxborough, Norfolk, England. This extremely rare bronze knife was too large and unwieldy to be a weapon, and was probably used for ceremonial purposes. (Photo: © British Museum)

material for blades. In fact the oldest known article of hammered iron is a Hittite dagger made before 1,350 BC that was found in Egypt. By 1,000 BC smelted iron was being extracted from terrestrial ore by using a higher temperature, a good air draft and a higher furnace to allow the mix of iron and slag to drop down from the smelting area.

Iron is twice as flexible as bronze; it is harder and much tougher. Even so, bronze was considered superior for ornamental and ceremonial blades, plus it was corrosion resistant, so there was considerable overlap between the Bronze and the Iron Ages in knifemaking.

The full development of the Iron Age came at around 700 BC when iron had become the material of choice for blade making throughout most of the civilized world. Yet even previously to this, by around 1,200 BC, it was discovered that iron could be hardened by adding carbon and heat-treating it to obtain a metal capable of retaining much superior edges. This was the first steel, and in time it was destined to replace all previous blade materials.

Right: Roman iron dagger and sheath, 1st century AD, found at a Roman Britain fort site at Hod Hill, Dorset, England. The dagger is of a type that may have been carried by Roman soldiers. The front plate of the iron sheath was often elaborately decorated – this example being based on rosettes and chevrons, picked out with inlays of brass and yellow enamel. (Photo: © British Museum)

Blade Materials

TWO THOUSAND YEARS AGO the art of blade making with steel had spread throughout the civilized world. Steel-bladed knives from around the first century BC onwards have been found in Italy, North Africa, the Middle East, Central and Northern Europe.

As smelting furnace construction technology advanced, steel became more common and less expensive. Eventually, steel was by far the most popular choice as a material for knife blades, a situation that continues right up to the present day.

Steel is iron which has been mixed with other essential elements, the main one being carbon – hence the term "carbon steel." The "blast furnace" fueled by charcoal (carbon) was in general use in parts of Asia by about the 7th century AD, in Europe by the 14th century, and in North America by 1620 (at Falling Creek, Virginia).

The more carbon that is added, the harder the steel will become and the better edge-holding properties the steel will have. It sounds simple enough, but there is an unfortunate side effect to adding carbon – the steel becomes more susceptible to corrosion. To counteract this problem, other elements are added.

In 1913, Harry Brearley of Sheffield, England, added chromium to carbon steel, which then underwent a stringent heating and finishing process to form an alloy that was highly resistant to corrosion. It became known as stainless steel, because it literally stained less.

Within a few years there were similar processes in the USA and Germany with nickel and chrome being added, and by the late 1920s stainless steel was being used for virtually all knifemaking, although some specialist knives (and notably some of the best French carving knives) are still made in carbon steel or carbon steel compounds.

MODERN STEELS

To obtain a good stainless steel a high amount of chromium (13-18 percent) is added to the iron ore. As edge-retention improves with a higher carbon content but can reduce with a high chromium content, other elements are introduced into the mix to aid this balancing act. These elements include nickel, manganese, molybdenum, silicon, tungsten and vanadium, added in various proportions either individually or in combinations.

Today there are many different types of steel available for blade making, and the choice can be confusing since each of them has different properties. In the main they fall into four categories:

Carbon steels: alloys of iron and carbon in varied proportion, but almost always over 0.5 percent carbon (known as a high carbon steel) for blade making.
Compound steels: carbon steels with additional elements but less than 13 percent chromium.
Stainless steels: carbon steels with other elements added, including at least 13 percent chromium.
Damascus steels: combinations of two different steels that are pattern-welded.

(Note: see the blade material chart for the most popular individual types of blade steel.)

Right: Unlike most modern pocket knives, Opinel folding knives are traditionally made with carbon steel blades – they are razor sharp, will hold an excellent edge and are easily sharpened. However, these inexpensive French knives are now available in stainless steel.

Above: *The Falkniven A2 "Wild Country" survival knife is made with an extremely sophisticated triple laminate stainless steel, made up of two layers of resilient 420J2 steel sandwiching hard VG10 steel which forms the blade's edge. This combination gives a strong, tough blade with excellent edge retention.*

Left: *The Chris Reeve "Project MkII" military style survival knife is made from one solid billet of A2 steel, an extremely tough, durable, tool grade steel that will take and retain a good edge, while still having reasonable resistance to corrosion.*

Although the choice of steel is important, it is what the individual knife maker or cutlery manufacturer does with it that determines how good the finished product turns out. The manufacturing process, special heat treatments and finishing, and even the shape of the blade are all factors in steel's performance.

One might think that a stainless steel would always be better than a plain carbon steel, but this is not the case. Carbon steels can be incredibly tough and offer all the qualities needed for a knife – easy to sharpen, a keen edge and good edge-retention. In fact, they can be better than some types of stainless steel.

The problem of carbon steel being susceptible to attack in the form of staining or corrosion (rusting) means that such blades need to be regularly maintained, by cleaning after use and protecting with light oil or a proprietary rust inhibitor when stowed (see the chapter on sharpening and maintenance). When talking of corrosion, we normally mean rust spotting (oxidization), which can be easily removed. This will only become serious, and turn into pitting, if the blade is neglected. Staining can occur when the blade comes into contact with certain acids or alkalis that can be commonly encountered. This occurs only with certain carbon steels and quite often it can be fairly easily removed, but in some cases staining can be stubborn. However, it rarely affects the usage of the knife, just the appearance.

The Cold Steel company use carbon steels in their Carbon V brand blades, while some KA-BAR knives are made of 1095 carbon steel (see blade materials chart), but both companies give these blades a protective coating to counter rust formation.

The steels referred to as "compound" in the blade material table are alloys of carbon steel and other elements, but they are not stainless steels, so must be looked after like ordinary carbon steels. These compound steel alloys were originally created for use in machine tools and other industrial applications. They are especially tough and are often chosen for military or "combat" knives. As stated above, stainless steels are by far the most popular materials for modern

blades...but not just any old stainless will do. Knifemakers have experimented long and hard to find steels that have the edge-holding and strength qualities of carbon steel combined with the corrosion-resistance of stainless steel. In the main they have succeeded, with materials such as 440C, AUS-10, 425-M and 12C-27 fulfilling most of the essential qualities required, and "super stainless steels" such as ATS-34 giving even better performance. There are many other grades, types and brands of stainless steels, each with stronger qualities in some areas, but weaker in others, that are being used by knifemakers for special applications.

It is important that you choose the right type of steel for the primary application for which you intend to use your knife. If your use involves heavy

Left: Many knives, such as this Frost hunting knife, are just marked "stainless steel," which usually means that they are made from one of the highly corrosion resistant 420 or 440 family of stainless steels, all of which have fairly high carbon and chrome contents.

Below: The blade on this Fred Carter designed knife by Gerber is made of AUS-8, a steel that is similar in its qualities and properties to 440B; easy to sharpen, good edge retention and high corrosion resistance.

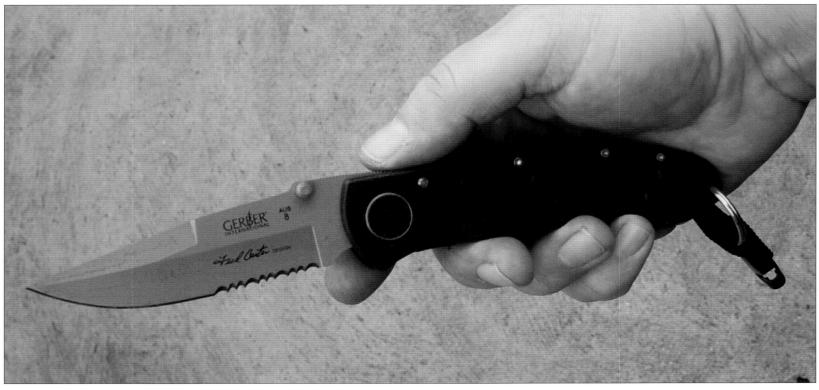

Below: This Blackie Collins designed Meyerco knife has a blade made of ATS-34, a Japanese made stainless steel that is generally regarded to be one of the finest available steels for knifemaking.

duty cutting on a regular basis, such as encountered by riggers, farmers or forestry workers, then a good carbon steel blade should be considered (note that continuous use is probably one of the best protections against corrosion problems). Hard compound steel alloys are the best choice for toughness, but not necessarily cutting ability. Stainless steels are the best "all-rounders," offering a blend of qualities that should suit most users. My advice is to go for a high chromium content if corrosion-resistance is the most important quality for you (such as in diving knives), or an above average carbon content if sharpness and edge-retention are your chief considerations. Pay just

a little extra for one of the super stainless steels (ATS-34, ATS-55, 154CM, RWL-34, etc.) for the best balance of qualities.

The other thing to remember is that despite its name, stainless steel can stain and rust – it is just a lot more resistant to attack by other elements because of its high chrome content. If your stainless knife is continuously exposed to corrosive elements, such as salt water, blood, citrus fruits or any other strong acid or alkaline sources, and it is not cleaned regularly, then you will get problems.

ROAD TO DAMASCUS...

Pattern-welded steel, also known as Damascene or Damascus steel, is another great material for knife blades, especially for the collector or connoisseur. It is one of the oldest forms of forged steel and, although it would seem that the process – of heating, folding and

Below: A modern Indian-made Damascus steel blade and tang made by pattern welding – the original "watered" steel from Damascus is said to have its origins in ancient Indian "Wootz" steel, the product of an alloying process now lost to history.

Above: Handmade hunting knife by Alan Wood with a 4" stainless steel Damascus blade in an Odin's Eye pattern – the handle is in African Blackwood, with Celtic style engraving on the bolster and pommel.

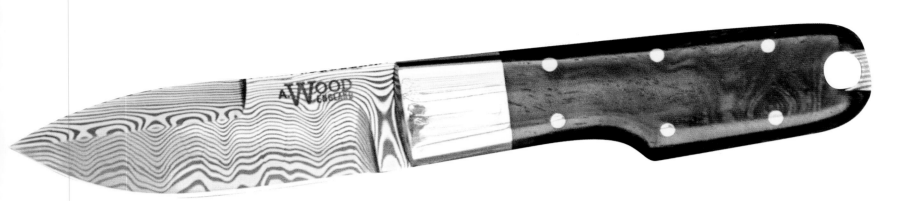

Above: Another custom made hunting knife from Alan Wood with a 2.5"
Damascus stainless steel blade, brass fittings and a "gunstock" style
cocobolo handle.

repeatedly beating out multiple layers of steels until the desired pattern is achieved – was known by many iron producing peoples (such as the Nordic and Japanese cultures), the modern name comes from the City of Damascus in the Persian Empire of 2,000 years ago. The city was famed for its steel sword blades which had a distinctive "watered" pattern of dark and light wavy lines. Yet there is a modern theory that these blades may have not been pattern-welded at all. Instead, it is claimed that watered Damascus steel may have been created by using "Wootz" steel, an alloy thought to have been made in India and then transported to Damascus in small billets or ingots. According to this theory it was then smelted, forged and cooled (not pattern-welded) in a special process which has been lost in history.

However, Damascus is now used to describe any steel that has been formed by laminating different steels by pattern-welding. By using this process a laminate of up to 500 layers can be created. The knifemaker can use various methods to fashion different patterns, such as twisting the steel, inlaying different metals, marking or drilling it, etc. Acid etching is also used to reveal and enhance the pattern. The resulting laminated steel, if competently created with the right materials, should be strong, great looking and hold an excellent edge.

Of course such a laborious and technically skilled process is bound to cost more than that used for ordinary steels, which is why hand-made Damascus blades are probably among the most expensive in the world.

It is also possible to manufacture Damascus steel on a larger scale and many knifemakers buy their stock material ready-formed. Just before this book went to press, I received a brochure on gun barrels formed from a superbly patterned material called Damasteel from Sweden. This is interesting stuff, since it is claimed to combine some of the top end stainless steels in a unique process. The barrels were available in a variety of patterns, and I understand that the same sort of steel is also available from this company as flat bar stock material for knife blades.

NON-FERROUS METALS AND SOME POTENT PLASTIC

Other materials used for knife blades include titanium, stellite, ceramics and various plastics. Titanium is famed for being as strong as steel but lighter in weight; unfortunately, it has also got a reputation for not taking an edge. Nevertheless, there are plenty of knifemakers willing to work with it, especially for top end of the market diving knives, since it has greater corrosion resistance than any steel. It is also used by Navy SEALs (SeaAirLand special forces) because it is not magnetic (the first titanium knife I ever saw was owned by a SEAL). Being used by such an elite military unit must be a great

Below: A Bird's Eye pattern Damascus carbon steel blade by Mick Wardell –
the handmade custom knife also has file work on the nickel silver guard, an
antler handle and scrimshaw pommel.

selling point on its own. Apparently, the latest titanium alloys will take a better edge than earlier titanium knives, and I've seen a few folders made from it, but it is a very expensive material to buy and difficult to work with.

One of the most unusual materials for blade making is stellite, a cobalt-based alloy claimed to have good edge-retention and near corrosion-free characteristics. As you might expect, it is usually associated with divers' knives, but even so it is rarely encountered.

Ceramic blades are more usually seen on fashionable kitchen cutlery, but a few ceramic sports knives are in production, including at least two from Boker's "Tree Brand." The blades usually come with a good edge that will last for ages, which is just as well, since some are sold with a recommendation to return them to the manufacturer for correct re-sharpening. Some pundits say that ceramic blades are too brittle and will shatter if dropped on a hard surface, but I've never come across anybody that has actually seen this happen.

The final main blade materials encountered are various types of plastic and nylon – remember, this is with regard to personal knives

Left: An unusual titanium folding knife handmade by British-based Persian knife-maker Farid. Titanium is a light, strong, corrosion free metal, but it is difficult to work with for blade making and quite expensive.

Below: This Tree Brand "Infinity" knife from German cutlery company Boker has a ceramic blade made by the Kyocera Corporation. Apparently the ceramic blade will stay sharp for an age.

Right: (top) The Cold Steel Special Projects Delta Dart, (bottom) the Cold Steel Special Projects Covert Action Tanto; both these "plastic knives" are made with Zytel glass fiber reinforced nylon, making them difficult to detect with some security screening systems.

as opposed to eating cutlery. These knives are often strengthened with molded reinforcing ribs and their cutting edges are made more effective by serrations. With the exception of the Lansky LS17, which could be used for minor cutting tasks, such as a box cutter or letter opener, the main purpose of plastic knives seems to be "self defense," hence they bear such names as the "Heart Attack Push Dagger." Another major selling point seems to be concealment or disguise, as with the "Stealth Defense" comb and brush, which both appear to be normal hairdressing tools but with a hidden reinforced plastic spike concealed in each of their handles.

Probably the best known of these plastic weapons are the Special Projects Delta Dart and Special Projects Covert Action Tanto, both made by Cold Steel. The first of these is a triangular bladed spike with a checkered grip and a round pommel that could be used in the style of a kubaton. The second looks like a black tanto with a "bevel ground" edge which might offer some cutting ability, but the angled chisel point looks as though it would be highly effective for piercing. Both of these items are made from Zytel, a glass-reinforced nylon.

THE ROCKWELL SCALE

The Rockwell C scale is used to measure the hardness of different grades of cutlery steel. A diamond point is pressed into the stock steel under the pressure of a low weight, then a much heavier weight, and finally the lighter weight again. The difference between the depth of the indents is measured and from the resulting calculation a comparison is made with the Rockwell scale. A broad average for usable knife steels starts at around 50 Rockwell right up to 60 Rockwell for a top end hard steel. Don't get too hung up on the Rockwell scale: it is of far more concern to the knifemaker than the knife user. Providing your knife falls within the usual parameters of hardness, there's not much to worry about.

Below: The LS-17 knife from Lansky Sharpeners is made entirely of black ABS plastic, making it light yet robust. A beveled edge and a small serrated section on the blade make it fairly useful for minor cutting tasks, but the spear-point design suggests that it lends itself more to use as an emergency weapon.

Blade Materials

The following steels and other materials are all used by major manufacturers and custom knifemakers. All such knifemakers have their own favorites for different tasks and some will swear by the blade materials listed, while others may swear at them! The list is representative, since there are far more steels available than we could possibly list here. Our object is to give you a simple guide, so that you know what to expect when you see it in a knife catalogue or actually marked on a knife blade.

CARBON STEELS

01: High carbon content gives an extremely sharp edge with excellent retention, but will corrode and discolor easily unless well maintained.

1095: A high carbon steel (0.95 percent carbon) from the 10 series of steels. It is fairly tough, sharpens easily and holds an edge well, but will rust if not well maintained.

COMPOUND STEELS

A-2: A tough tool steel, very strong; will take a good edge and retain it. Reasonable to sharpen and having fair corrosion resistance. Chris Reeve uses A2 for his extremely robust military knives.

D-2: Very hard and extremely strong tool steel. Can be difficult to sharpen but will hold a usable edge for an age. It does have a fairly high chrome content, so it is more corrosion resistant than many compound steels, but it's not stainless.

M-2: Another tough tool steel that will hold a good edge, but not as commonly seen as A-2 or D-2. Will rust if not maintained.

Below: Sheet stock D2 tool steel is used for the blade of the KA-BAR D2; this steel is massively tough and will maintain a good edge through a lot of hard use, but it is prone to corrosion, which is one reason that this blade is epoxy coated apart from the edge.

STAINLESS STEELS

Above: 154CM steel is similar in composition and quality to ATS-34, making it one of the finest steels for knife making – Spyderco use it on several of their knives including the Trakker.

Above: British Army utility knife in stainless steel by J.Adams of Sheffield – surgical grade stainless steels are used for most knife applications and are usually 440A, 440B, 440C, or similar types, such as AUS-6, AUS-8, AUS-10, or 12C-27.

Above: This unusual looking C80 Spyderco uses CPM S30V, an innovative high grade cutlery steel from Crucible Particle Metallurgy, a company on the "cutting edge" of specialist steel development.

ATS-34 and 154CM: Excellent blade steels with very similar compositions; both offer good corrosion resistance, take a good edge and retain it well. When the edge does go it may take a little effort and patience to get right. Generally accepted as the very best stainless steels for blades.

ATS-55: A relatively new steel that is supposed to be like ATS-34 but without molybdenum (which shouldn't affect its qualities as a blade making material, but should make it cheaper); takes an excellent edge.

BG-42: Another new steel to knifemaking. I am not familiar with it, but it is said to be equal to or better than ATS-34. Some big names in custom made knives are starting to use it.

CPM 440V and CPM 420V: These are two steels made by a process called Crucible Particle Metallurgy (CPM), which basically means reducing the component elements to a

Above: Even though this Colt Python knife has a 440 stainless steel blade, the manu-facturers have chosen to give it a black epoxy coating. This is not just "cosmetic" as coated steel blades are often used in military applications to make them less reflective.

Right: These Spyderco Impala knives – by Ed Scott from South Africa – have blades made of VG10, a superior grade steel with high levels of molybdenum and cobalt for toughness.

powder then combining and compressing them before return-ing to a "solid" state. Although reckoned to be difficult to sharpen, such knives come with a good reputation for holding an edge and corrosion resistance. Spyderco have started to use these metals.

CPMS30V: This is a brand new CPM steel, said to be very tough and corrosion resistant. Apparently already being used by Chris Reeve in some folding knives.

G-2 or GIN-1: Similar in blade properties to ATS-34, and as such offers good corrosion resistance and edge qualities. Used by Spyderco for some applications.

RWL-34: An advanced version of ATS-34 steel but with an increased edge strength and better edge-holding consistency. Used by UK custom knife maker Alan Wood.

440C (also AUS-10): Surgical grade quality and one of the most popular steels for knifemaking. Stainless qualities are good, it will take and retain a good edge, and is easy to sharpen. The industry benchmark before ATS-34 and still by far the knifemaker's favorite.

440A and 440B: Both very strong steels, with high carbon and high chrome content, similar qualities to 440C but not as hard (less carbon) although they both have more effective resistance to corrosion.

AUS-6, AUS-8, 425-M (modified) and Sandvik 12C-27: High carbon, high chrome, good corrosion resistance; they sharpen easily and hold their edge. Good all round choice. Fairly similar in properties to 440A and 440B. Used in some applications by KA-BAR.

420: A general grade steel with average edge-retaining capabilities, but it has excellent stainless qualities. Sometimes used for diving knives and presentation knives, but also found on economy lines.

VG10: Another relatively new top quality steel, with a higher molybdenum content than Gin-1 and the addition of a high (approx 1.4 percent) amount of cobalt – much higher than ATS-55. These elements should help make the steel tougher, harder, but not brittle. Now being used on some Spyderco models and extensively by Fallkniven.

Above: The Nordic series of knives from use blades of Sandvik 12c-27 steel, a Swedish surgical grade stainless steel.

PATTERN-WELDED (DAMASCUS) STEELS

Damascus (carbon steel): A pattern-welded blend of two carbon steels. Not common, but will generally have good edge qualities and will also look good. Corrosion resistance will not be as good as a stainless steel and it will probably be more expensive.

Damascus (stainless steel): Properties can vary depending on the types of steel used in its forming, but will usually have excellent edge-retention qualities, corrosion resistance, and is one of the most attractive steels; but it is far more expensive than single stainless steels.

San Mai III: This is the trade name from knife manufacturers Cold Steel for a three-layer laminate steel in the Japanese style ("San Mai" actually means "three layers"). The center layer is a hard, high-carbon steel for a good edge, while the outer layers are lower in carbon for a flexible but tougher blade.

NON-FERROUS MATERIALS (NOT IRON BASED)

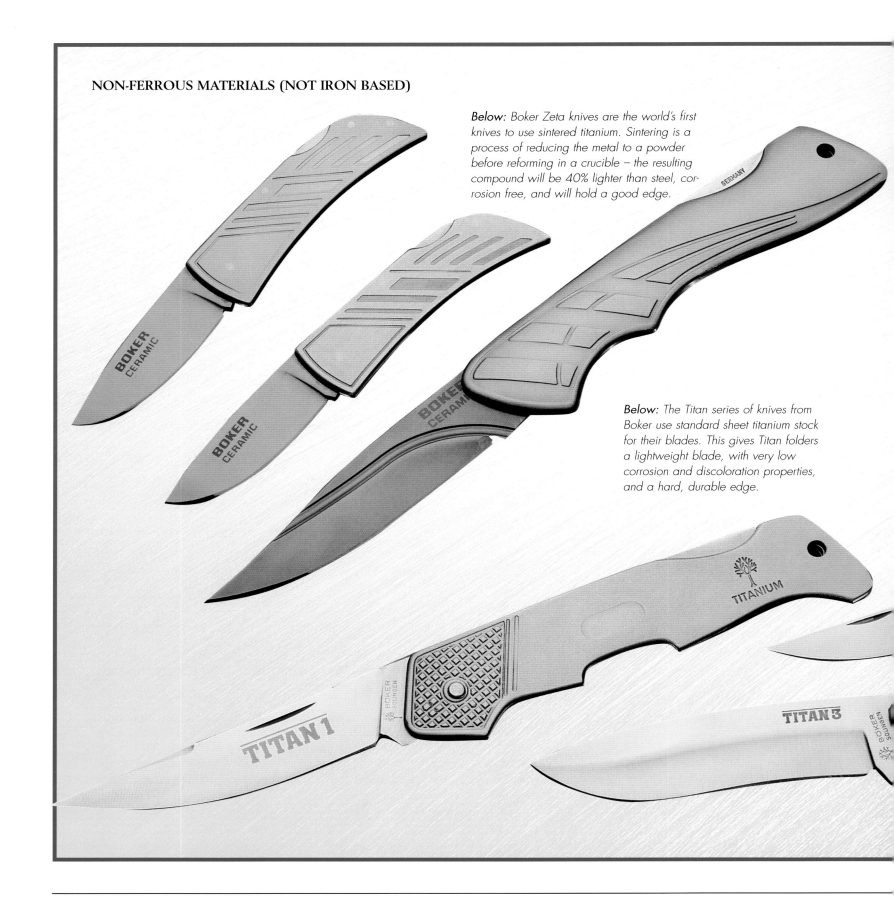

Below: Boker Zeta knives are the world's first knives to use sintered titanium. Sintering is a process of reducing the metal to a powder before reforming in a crucible – the resulting compound will be 40% lighter than steel, corrosion free, and will hold a good edge.

Below: The Titan series of knives from Boker use standard sheet titanium stock for their blades. This gives Titan folders a lightweight blade, with very low corrosion and discoloration properties, and a hard, durable edge.

Ceramics: This material is rarely used in field knives, but it is harder than steel, usually comes with a fairly good edge, and will hold it through a lot of usage.

Plastics: These can be any of a number of stiff plastic or nylon materials, sometimes reinforced with glass-fiber. Usually used to make serrated edged box cutters and spike-like "self-defense" daggers.

Stellite: This is the commercial name for an almost corrosion-free, hard-wearing alloy material based mainly on cobalt, chromium and tungsten. Rarely used except in a few custom and diving knives.

Talonite: Another cobalt-based alloy, with chromium and molybdenum. Is claimed to be very tough, extremely corrosion resistant, will take a good edge and is "slicker" than other blade materials. Expensive and rare, but now being used by Camillus in their Talonite Quest and Mini Talon knives.

Titanium: A light and strong metal, almost corrosion-free and non-magnetic. It had a bad reputation for not taking an edge, but apparently the latest alloys are much better. Expensive.

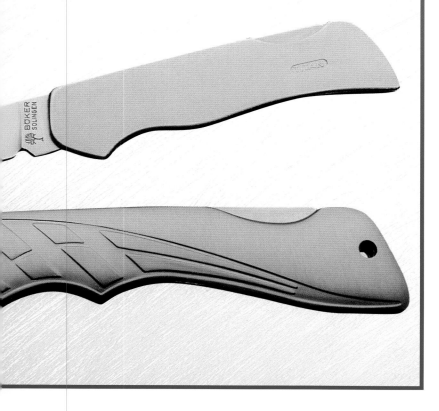

FIXED OR FOLDING?

One of the most important aspects of a knife's blade is whether it should be fixed or folding. The structure of a fixed blade knife is totally different from that of a folder. Fixed blades have the potential to be much stronger, since the central part of the handle – the "tang" – is an extension of the blade itself. On the other hand, the handle of a folder can be quite a complex structure, with the blade joined to it only by an axis pin, upon which the blade can be swiveled to the open or closed position. This does not mean that folding knives are inherently weak; it's just that more thought has to go into their construction to make them as strong as ordinary fixed blade knives.

The main features of the fixed blade knife are its simple design and construction, its potential for great strength and the fact that it can be made in large sizes with few problems. The minus points are that for an equivalent blade size it is roughly twice the length of a folding knife when being transported (since a folder would be in the closed position). Because the fixed blade knife always shows its bared edge, for obvious safety reasons it has to be kept sheathed when not in use or when being carried. This too can have its problems, because in many countries even the carrying of a fixed blade knife – in a sheath or not – can be either illegal or considered socially unacceptable, except in certain special circumstances (such as when carried by agricultural or other rural workers).

The biggest disadvantage with folding knives is that they need to be well constructed to be as strong as a fixed blade. This usually means extra expense. The folder has to have a lock of some sort to hold the blade open, and no matter how well a lock is made there is the possibility that it will fail under adverse circumstances. It is much more likely to occur through owner misuse or neglect. This can be particularly true with long-bladed knives, where extra strain is caused through leverage on the blade's pivot or axis pin, especially if subjected to forces applied from the side against the flat of the blade. This is one reason that there is a finite limit to the sensible length of blade that you can have with a folding knife. Usually, the longer the blade, the longer the handle has to be to accommodate it, although some Spanish knife-makers put this rule to the test with giant versions of their traditional navaja knife.

The best feature of the "folding blade" knife is just that…. The blade can be folded away and safely stowed in the handle. This halves the size of the knife when the blade is not in use, making it a far more convenient tool to carry. The folder's moderate size means that it is often adapted to a variety of different tasks – some probably better tackled with a fixed blade knife – but the folder is more convenient in modern urban society. The average sized folding knife can generally be carried in your pocket (hence the term "pocket knife"!), even though many owners choose to carry them in a purpose designed belt pouch, or on a spring clip, or with a shackle and dog clip (snap clip). So despite their apparent disadvantages, folding knives remain extremely popular because of their convenience, versatility and social acceptability, while fixed blade knives are prized for their strength, toughness and, for certain uses the blade size.

Fixed Blade Knives

The Fixed Blade Knife

This is a composite diagram intended to show the various parts of fixed blade knives. It is based on the design features of several different knives, but you will never find all these features on any "single" knife.

KEY:

A. A metal finishing piece for the handle is usually called a "pommel" if solid or a "cap" if hollow – but some knives have neither.

B. Rivet, pin or bolt to attach the grip scales or handle to the knife's tang.

C. One piece handle or two grip 'scales' (one either side of the tang).

D. A finger grip (for extra control) sometimes confusingly called a choil (see below). There may be up to four finger grips on a handle or there may be none at all.

E. A quillon – this is a metal extension forming part of the guard. It may be on one or both sides of the guard and can be straight or curved.

F. The choil is a cut-out indent on the blade, usually big enough for a finger on a fixed blade knife, but often just a "nick" on a folding knife.

G. The edge. This is usually formed by grinding a primary bevel (angle) on both sides of the blade "flat" to gradually reduce the thickness of the metal and then a secondary bevel to actually make the sharp edge.

H. The "belly" is the curve from the lowest point of the blade to the tip.

I. The point or tip of the blade where the belly and spine meet.

J. The "clip" – a curved cut-away found on some blades. The concave edge can be a swedge (beveled or swaged but unsharpened) or it can be sharpened (in which case it is termed a "false edge").

K. The "fuller" is a hollowed channel on the blade "flat". More commonly found on swords it is seen on very few modern knives. Its other common name is "blood-let", but it's real purpose was to remove metal, therefore lightening the blade.

L. The "spine" is the unsharpened back edge of the knife.

M. The "shoulder" marks the boundary between the flat ricasso and the beveled edge of the blade.

N. The "ricasso" is a flat unbeveled part of the blade between the tang and the edged portion of the blade.

O. The guard is a shaped metal plate between the blade and the handle to protect the user's hand.

P. The "bolster" is a strengthening metal component between blade and handle.

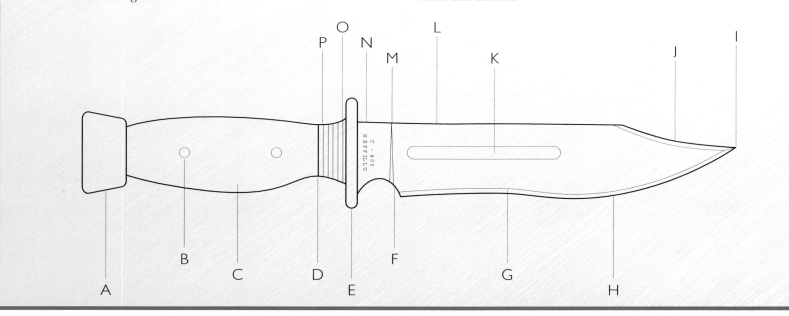

THIS CHAPTER is intended to be a broad guide to fixed blade knives, their designs, component parts and specific properties. You will find many overlaps between the types and their names; even manufacturers can confuse the issue by labeling virtually identical knives differently…. One man's drop point blade can be another man's utility knife – but, as always, it is the ability to do the job that really counts.

Just because a knife is not labeled "skinner" does not mean that you can't skin with it. Likewise, a skinning knife can be used for lots of other cutting tasks. Nevertheless, if you know what your knife will mainly be used for, the following information should help you in choosing a suitable blade type.

The two main jobs for knives are cutting and piercing. The blade is used to cut and the point is used to pierce. But there is a lot more to it than that.

Cutting can be classified into fine (food slicing and preparation, whittling, etc.), general (rope work, skinning and field dressing, etc.) and heavy (chopping hard materials, hacking through vegetation, large game jointing, etc.). There are dozens of other applications and a large margin of cross-over between many of them, but if your main knife use falls squarely into one of them, then you can refine your

Left: Traditionally styled large bowie knife with 13.5" clip point blade (18.5" overall length, 23oz in weight) by Mick Wardell.

Below: Seven fixed blade hunting/skinning knives by Mick Wardell – all these knives are of full tang construction with various types of wood grip scales, they have no guards, bolsters or separate pommels.

Above: Graham Holbrook handmade hunting dirk with superbly finished 12c27 steel blade, leather and stag antler handle with brass guard and butt cap.

choice of blade considerably.

Apart from use as a weapon, the piercing power of a knife's point rarely comes into use, apart from starting a cutting or skinning task, to bore a hollow or hole in a hard material or to pierce a softer sheet material, like leather or canvas. All these factors should be borne in mind when choosing your knife.

TWO-PART HARMONY

At its most basic the fixed blade knife is made up of just two main parts; the blade and the handle. Yet if you browse through any knife catalog or outdoor store you will see hundreds of different knives; large and small, general-purpose or specialist, mass-produced or

handmade…. The list could go on and on, but they are all based on that same two-part concept. They may have any one of a dozen or so main blade types – depending on the intended use – and there are scores of different materials that could be chosen for the handle. In addition they might be fitted with a cross-guard, bolster or pommel, or a combination of these or other features, but their strength – literally – is in their two-part structure.

THE TANG

When most people talk about blades they are actually referring to that sharp-pointed bit sticking out of the handle – naturally enough – but at the other end of the blade there is the "tang," which is equally important. The term tang is used to describe the portion of the blade that extends into the handle and acts as an internal frame with which to join these two major components together.

There are four main types of tang: the full tang; the half tang; the

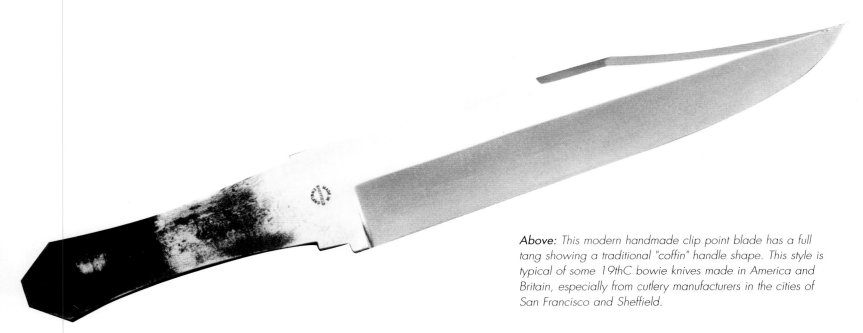

Above: *This modern handmade clip point blade has a full tang showing a traditional "coffin" handle shape. This style is typical of some 19thC bowie knives made in America and Britain, especially from cutlery manufacturers in the cities of San Francisco and Sheffield.*

rat tail tang; the push tang. My understanding of a full tang is a flat un-sharpened part of the blade that forms the actual shape of the handle, which is completed by attaching grip scales to both sides (usually with rivets) and, in some cases, a pommel and/or bolster to either end of the handle. It is one of the strongest of all knife designs, since even if the scales are destroyed or damaged the central steel core of the handle remains with its shape intact.

However, some commercial knife makers describe any metal projection that runs from the ricasso to the end of the handle as a full tang, no matter what shape it is. The correct term for such knives, depending on type, can be worked out from the definitions below, but they are not full tangs. So if you want a knife with a real full tang, take a look at the edge of the handle. If you see metal sandwiched between the two grip scales for the whole of their length, then you have a full tang knife.

A half tang is literally that – half a full tang. It follows the shape of the handle for half it's length, but instead of two grip scales it usually has a slotted one-piece handle. This slides over the tang and, as

Below: *A selection of blades from Swedish knife manufacturers Brusletto, showing various types of tangs; (left to right) long push tang with lug, half tang, drilled push tang, rounded rat tail tang, tapered rat tail tang, squared rat tail tang, tapered rat tail, wavy push tang, half tang, hidden push tang.*

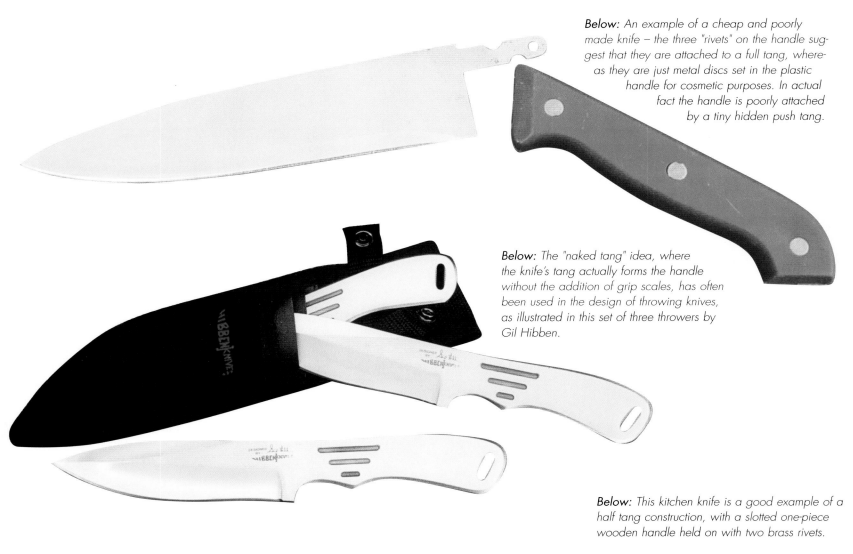

Below: An example of a cheap and poorly made knife – the three "rivets" on the handle suggest that they are attached to a full tang, whereas they are just metal discs set in the plastic handle for cosmetic purposes. In actual fact the handle is poorly attached by a tiny hidden push tang.

Below: The "naked tang" idea, where the knife's tang actually forms the handle without the addition of grip scales, has often been used in the design of throwing knives, as illustrated in this set of three throwers by Gil Hibben.

Below: This kitchen knife is a good example of a half tang construction, with a slotted one-piece wooden handle held on with two brass rivets.

with the full tang, is usually attached with rivets or pins.

The rat tail tang is a narrow, straight or tapered strip of steel that can be round, square or rectangular in section, and extends from the blade through the center of the handle. If the rat tail is round the end is usually threaded and attaches to a one-piece drilled handle via a nut. Alternatively, if the tail is square or rectangular, the base can be drilled and threaded to take a bolt or screw.

The rat tail is one of the most popular ways of attaching a handle and is used on some very good knives, including many of the very best chef's knives and some custom-made blades. The design is robust, but relies a little more than other tangs on the inherent strength of whatever handle material is being used.

The push tang is a narrow strip of flat steel that extends from the blade and is "pushed" into the handle. Sometimes it has one or two holes to accept rivets, while other examples have notches or lugs that will engage similar projections or depressions inside the handle. The latter type is often found on modern knives with slim gauge steel blades and molded plastic handles. These tangs can be of any length, but when they are less than half as long as the handle they are sometimes referred to as partial, encapsulated or hidden push tangs. The push tang is used extensively on stamped blades and, although probably the least expensive method of joining blade to handle, for applications where great strength is not required they can still do an acceptable job.

Apart from these four main types of tang, there is one other design that is gaining in popularity, the skeleton or naked tang. On this design there are no grip scales or "handle" at all, since the tang itself forms the whole of the handle. Some of these tangs are solid, while others are more like a hollow frame. The owner can use the knife as it comes, or alternatively wrap the tang/frame with paracord or affix other materials to form a custom grip.

In all but the last of the examples above, the tang is concealed by the handle, but on many knives there is often a small, visible unbeveled section of the blade between the tang and the sharpened edge. This is called the ricasso. This part of the blade is often stamped with information about the maker, country of origin and type of steel used. The edge side border of the ricasso is defined by a step – known as a "shoulder" – down to the beveled section of the blade that actually forms the edge.

Below: Some knives come with a hollow uncovered tang, giving a "skeleton" grip which can be left as it is or covered with the owner's choice of handle or grip scale if desired – this particular model is the CRKT Stiff KISS tanto with a nylon cord grip attached by the author.

Fixed Blade Shapes

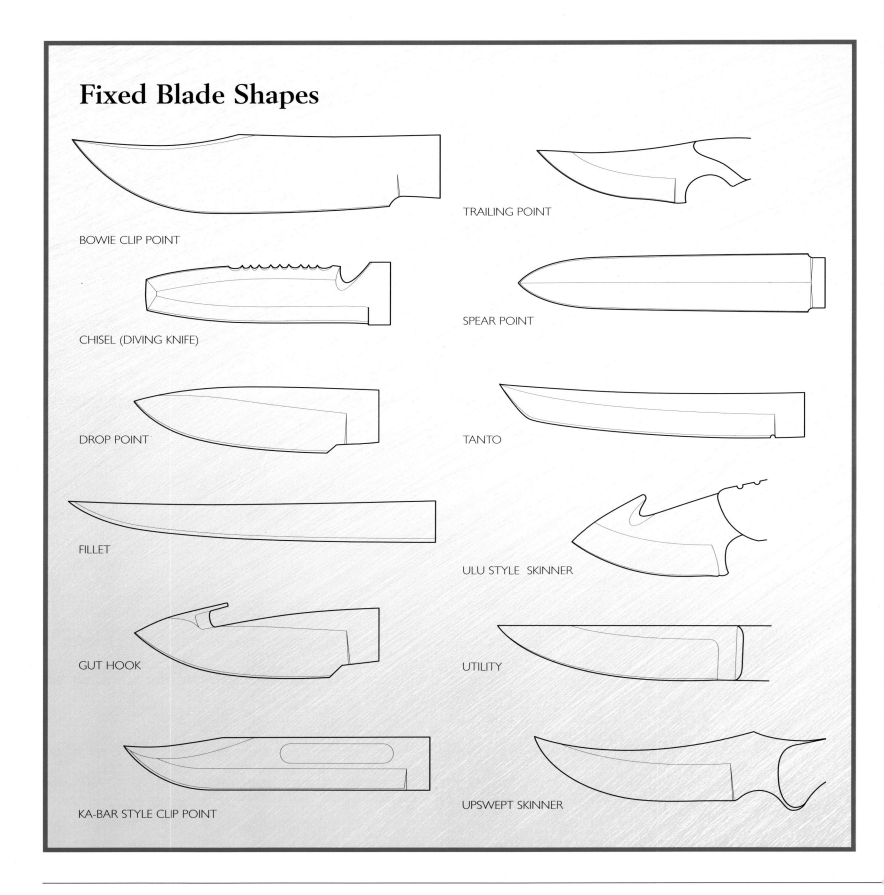

BOWIE CLIP POINT

CHISEL (DIVING KNIFE)

DROP POINT

FILLET

GUT HOOK

KA-BAR STYLE CLIP POINT

TRAILING POINT

SPEAR POINT

TANTO

ULU STYLE SKINNER

UTILITY

UPSWEPT SKINNER

GETTING INTO SHAPE

When choosing a knife one of the most important decisions to be made is what sort of blade is required. This obviously depends on the particular type of work that will regularly be done with it, but there are a few blade designs that can prove suitable for a number of different tasks. In fact there are only about a dozen practical fixed blade designs, but each one of them has a dozen variations and each maker will add his own ideas and nuances. Here are the main types that you are likely to come across;

CHISEL POINT

This is a specialized design, not to be confused with a chisel edge grind, as found on American-style tantos (see below). The chisel point is not a point at all; it's a squared-off end, often with an unsharpened bevel, and its specific purpose, unlike the point on any other knife you will come across, is as a pry-bar. For this reason it is

usually found only on knives designed for use by divers, mountaineers or emergency rescue services.

CLIP POINT

The embodiment of the classic clip point shape is seen on the bowie knife. In fact, when found on a fixed blade knife, a clip point is often referred to as a "bowie" blade. This is an old design, but it is still one of the most popular choices for an all-round outdoor knife. The clip point blade is sharpened on one side only, ended in a sweeping convex curve up to the point, giving a long curved "belly" for a powerful cutting stroke. The spine side of the blade has a shallow concave or straight cut-out leading to the tip – this is the "clip." This brings the blade point lower than the spine for a sharper tip, although some models have such an upswept clip that the tip actually ends up higher than the spine – more like an upswept skinner (see below). The lower point also helps to give better control when using the knife for skinning or fine point work. The clip may either have a false edge (a

Below: Custom made bowie with a typical clip point blade. This particular knife was handmade by Irish bladesmith, Rory Conner; note also the guard with single quillon.

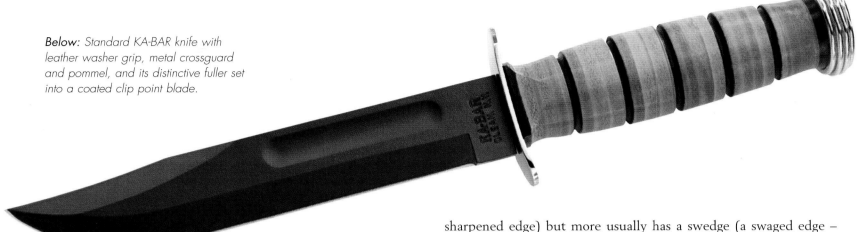

Below: Standard KA-BAR knife with leather washer grip, metal crossguard and pommel, and its distinctive fuller set into a coated clip point blade.

sharpened edge) but more usually has a swedge (a swaged edge – beveled but unsharpened). One of the most famous modern versions of the clip point blade can be found on the KA-BAR military knife, but there are dozens of other variations on the theme.

DROP POINT

The drop point is undoubtedly one of the most popular blade styles and certainly the most versatile, being capable of handling a multitude of cutting tasks from field dressing a deer carcass, through to general slicing and cutting. The drop point blade has a shallow convex curve coming down from the unsharpened spine to the point,

Below: The drop point is regarded by many as the best all-round blade shape for a hunting knife – this particular knife is designed by Bill Moran and is one of the few fixed blade models made by Spyderco.

Above: This Buck Alpha Hunter knife has a fixed guthook blade – a specialist skinning style that is becoming increasingly popular with deerstalkers and other hunters.

Below: Outdoor Edge fillet knives with upswept serrated blades and unusual T bar handles.

where it then meets the sharpened edge that rises up from the knife's belly in a deeper curve. The result is a slightly lower tip, falling between the spine and the centerline of the blade flat. This gives good control and minimal risk of underlying tissue damage during fine skinning work, while the fairly deep belly is sufficient for general skinning and gutting, with enough straight edge for jointing. These features also make the drop point one of the "handiest" blades for all types of other work and, because of its relatively simple lines, it is also one of the easiest to sharpen. The drop point described above is the type of blade made famous by world-renowned knife designer Bob Loveless, but there is another fairly distinct version with a longer blade in addition to shallower downward and upward curves from the spine and the belly, resulting in a much more slender-looking knife with a very keen point.

FILLET

This is a specialist tool, but it is included here because so many knives of this type are sold and are currently in use throughout the world. The filleting blade is long and slim, with an extremely sharp single-edged blade that comes to a fine point that is often curved slightly upwards, and – most importantly – it is very flexible. Used specifically for gutting, cleaning and filleting fish, the blade has to flex in order to follow the natural lines of the fish's anatomy. Even so, it is often pressed into service for general cutting work by fisherman, but it is not usually stiff enough for really heavy duty use.

GUTHOOK

Another specialist blade, this is a tool for the hunter and its primary use is skinning, gralloching (gutting) and the general field dressing of a carcass. The shape can best be described as a drop point but modified with the addition of a sharpened "V" or "U" shaped notch on the back edge (the spine) of the blade's tip. This gives the characteristic "hook" appearance – hence the name. In use, a small incision is made in the skin of the carcass to be dressed, then the blade is reversed (spine first) and the gut hook is inserted and carefully pulled along, cutting through the skin but with less danger of piercing the gut and contaminating the meat. The short back edge of the gut hook is usually wider and flatter than a normal knife spine to give a blunt cutting guide – just rest it on the first layer of flesh to protect the carcass from damage when "unzipping" the skin.

SKINNER (CAPER)

Originally designed for extremely close control work, such as intricate skinning (as in caping a beast's head), this design has become progressively shorter and deeper in profile, and is now becoming the hunting knife of choice for many modern deer stalkers and game hunters. Think of a laterally compressed drop point design with a short, gently curved (convex) spine meeting a deeply curved edged belly at the point, and you more or less have it. Don't be fooled by the compact size: used correctly this knife type will dress fairly large game. Columbia River Knife & Tool (CRKT) make a version of this knife called the "Cobuk" Skinner, designed by Alaskan knifemaker and hunting guide Russ Kommer for skinning game as large as caribou (in fact, cobuk is an Inuit word for caribou).

SKINNER (RADICAL)

This is a skinning and gralloching knife that pretty much takes the idea of an upswept skinner (see below) to the absolute limit with an exaggerated upswept blade. There are many different versions of this type of knife, some with offset handles to increase the slicing capabilities even more. The point is often needle sharp (sometimes with a false edged clip on the spine), but the upswept angle can make it awkward to use for most practical tasks. Some of these blades also have finger holes and/or milled edges on the spine to aid close control when being used for fine dressing work.

I once mildly criticized one of these knives (the Frost Wild Cat) in print, because the radical shape of the blade and handle set-up pretty much restricted the user to one type of grip. I suggested this

Below: The CRKT Alaska Carcajou Hunter is an all-round knife with a utility blade for both hunting and fishing use designed by Alaskan guide, Russ Kommer.

Above: The Russ Kommer Cobuk knife is also made by Columbia River Knife & Tool, but it has a deeper blade more suited to skinning large game from Whitetail deer to Alaskan moose. Skinning and caping knives used to be fairly slim, but now these short deep blade designs are becoming more popular.

Right: This throwing knife by Gil Hibben has an exaggerated spear point blade, with edges ground into both sides tapering into a point and strengthened by a central rib.

was not the ideal situation when unzipping and paunching rabbits. A big game hunter sent me a letter stating in no uncertain terms that the Wild Cat was one of the best knives he had ever used for skinning a polar bear! My point, however, is that the knife in question may be one of the best available for skinning bears, but I didn't rate it for bunnies – besides, you don't find many bears in my part of England. This was clearly a case of the wrong knife for the job.

SKINNER (UPSWEPT)
Typically this blade shape falls between the radical skinner (see above) and the trailing point (see below). It has a long, upswept edge

Below: The Wild Cat by Frost is a radical skinner that is designed in such a way that it can only be used in one grip position, which is quite restrictive, yet it still has its fans.

terminating in a fine point that is higher than the spine, which in turn has a shallow concave profile. The purpose of this is to give a long cutting edge with a point that is kept high and safely out of the way when skinning. The tip end of the spine can be either beveled (swaged) or plain. The trouble with this design is that the upward sweep of the point can make it quite difficult to use – and you are pretty much restricted to just one method of use. On the other hand, I know people that love this blade style – it's just one of those designs that you will either swear by or swear at. Although this blade could be used as a general-purpose design, it is not as versatile as the clip point or the trailing point, both of which have most of the upswept skinner's best qualities and neither of its faults.

SPEAR POINT

Used mainly in military or self-defense applications, the keen point on this symmetrical design lines up exactly with the center of the flat of the blade, and both edges are usually sharpened from the tip to the ricasso (or guard if there is no ricasso). The concept is probably as old as the Stone Age and the idea is that it offers good piercing potential with the ability to wound with a forward, upward or downward thrust, and with a lateral or a reverse sweep (a slashing motion). The spear point can obviously be used for duties other than fighting, but it is not the best shape for general cutting work, although – more often than not – in practice that is exactly what it does get used for, and few examples of the type ever get used for the

purpose envisaged by their designers (thankfully).

If the edge on one side of a spear point is sharpened only from the tip to about a third of the way down the blade, the design is usually classified separately as a "saber point." If a spear point is exceptionally long and narrow, it is usually referred to as a stiletto, but it is unusual to find modern fixed blade stilettos for civilian use, although they were quite common in the distant past.

Knives made for the sport of knife-throwing are often made with modified spear point styling, except that they have fairly swollen bellies on both sides of the knife. The idea of this is to aid balance and help give a straightening "keel" effect as the knife travels through the air, while also helping to limit penetration of the target.

TANTO

There are a number of quite different modern blade shapes that various manufacturers describe as "tanto." Basically they all originally stem from an old Japanese design with a sinuous curved blade featuring a shallow grind on both sides of a single edge. The more popular "American tanto" differs in that it usually has a chisel grind on just one side of the edge and the knife has a much more angular look. The chisel edge blade is usually straight and runs in parallel with the spine for most of its length, before sharply angling upwards in a straight line at around 45 degrees to form the point. This design creates a very sharp edge with a strong cutting point, lining up directly with the spine for very effective penetration capability. Quite a few companies have adapted the tanto styling for some military knife applications; probably just as much for its highly marketable looks as much as its tactical qualities.

TRAILING POINT

This type of knife is very similar to the upswept skinner, but the blade's point is only slightly higher than the spine. This still gives a long curved edge, but without the virtually unusable point (in my

Above: Japanese style tanto blades are becoming increasingly popular – this Master Samurai tanto, handmade by Farid, is 19" long overall, with a cord bound handle dipped in clear resin.

opinion) of the upswept skinner. Although primarily a skinning knife, the less radical shape of the trailing point can be pressed into use for most general cutting tasks, and a well made example can make a passable all-round outdoor knife.

UTILITY
As the name suggests, this is a general-purpose outdoor knife. It has no really outstanding features and no real faults – it is just a good

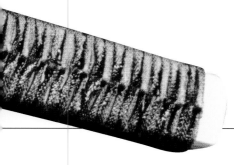

Above: Variations on a theme – three different blade types on knives from different countries, yet they are remarkably similar; the Bison from Great Britain has a utility blade, the Swedish Nordic is a drop point, and the Spanish made Joker has a modified spear point blade.

solid workhorse, and that's no bad thing.

The utility knife generally has a straight spine meeting a long curve from the edged belly of the knife. This gives it a long cutting edge and a useable point – it is a very similar design to a chef's paring knife.

Sometimes the spine of the knife has a barely noticeable convex curve running down to the tip, effectively turning the knife into a kind of shallow drop point. I like this design more than the version with the perfectly straight spine. This preference, however, is purely a matter of personal choice.

Edge Grinds

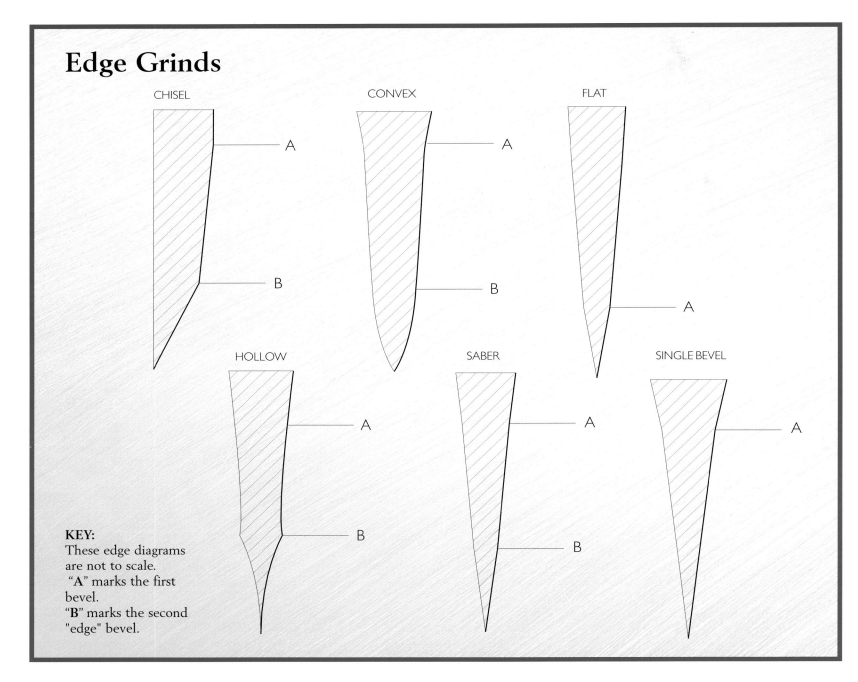

CHISEL

A

B

CONVEX

A

B

FLAT

A

A

HOLLOW

A

B

SABER

A

B

SINGLE BEVEL

A

KEY:
These edge diagrams
are not to scale.
"**A**" marks the first
bevel.
"**B**" marks the second
"edge" bevel.

THE CUTTING EDGE

Generally speaking, knives are usually ground with two angles – the first removes stock material from the blade flats to form the primary bevel, then a much smaller secondary bevel forms the actual edge. This secondary bevel usually concerns the knife owner most, as this is usually the part that he will have to re-sharpen at intervals. Even so, the primary bevel should also be considered, since the way it is ground by the manufacturer can have a great bearing on the performance of a knife. The primary bevel can be ground in a number of ways, the following examples are the main ones that you likely to encounter.

CHISEL
As described above in the tanto blade profile, this grind is on one side only, usually starting from the middle line of the blade down to the secondary bevel, while the other side of the blade is left completely flat from spine to edge. This makes the blade extremely sharp – and easy to re-sharpen – but some critics say it requires more attention than a double-sided grind because the edge is too thin and

fragile, especially in tough, prolonged cutting tasks. I've never found this myself, but then I've never subjected one to really heavy use, as I am not a great fan of the type for general cutting work.

CONVEX

As the name suggests, the two sides of the blade are ground in convex curves to form the edge – there are no secondary bevels with this grind. This profile is mainly chosen for its great strength, but it can also give a very sharp edge, obviously depending on the angle of the curves. It sounds like a good design – and it is – but it can be notoriously difficult to re-sharpen correctly.

HOLLOW

This consists of two concave grind profiles, one on each side of the blade. This gives a very fine and extremely sharp edge with high-performance cutting and slicing capabilities. The downside is that because the edge is thin, it is prone to chipping (especially if the knife is used for high impact work such as chopping) and "rolling" (when the fine edge is rolled over, usually due to excessive force or poor technique when cutting hard materials). The "straight" or "cut throat" razor is a good example of a hollow ground blade.

FLAT

This is one of the simplest grinds – and one of the best. It consists of a narrow angled flat grind on both sides of the blade, running from the spine right down to the secondary bevels. This allows a formidably sharp edge to be produced and it is also reasonably strong. Some of the very best chef's and butcher's knives are made to this format. The main drawback is expense, since a lot of material has to be ground away to form this profile and not all steels will take the design well.

Below: Italian made Extreme Ratio "Col.Moschin" military style combat knife with a semi serrated edge, cobalt steel blade and kraton handle.

SABER

This is similar to the flat grind, except that the primary bevels start at the middle of the blade. The secondary bevel used with this grind is also often less acute, giving a very strong durable edge with a reasonable level of sharpness. There are no really bad points to this edge profile; it is just that it is more suited to heavy-duty cutting and chopping – rather than as a fine cutter and slicer. This grind is often chosen for military and general camp knives.

SERRATED

This is where the edge of the blade is configured in a number of ridges, sometimes in two different sizes grouped in sequence along the blade. Usually these ridges or serrations are chisel ground straight through to the edge with no secondary grind, making this whole "train" of edges extremely sharp. This makes for a very effective cutting edge as a whole, because the high points on the serrations tend to momentarily "grab and puncture" the material – starting the cut – then the "train" of razor sharp edges along the steel just rips through. Because the serrations are ground on both their peaks and troughs there is good cutting power in both forward and reverse strokes – a sawing action. A serrated blade will also remain an effective slicer even after a lot of cutting work, simply because of its shape, but when it does need sharpening it can take a lot of time and patience. For some reason the serrated edge has never caught on for fixed blade sporting knives, although some modern designs now include a small section of serrations on the spine or the edge, usually just in front of the ricasso or guard.

SINGLE BEVEL

This grind starts from the middle of the blade then runs right down to the edge and, as the name suggests, there are no secondary edge bevels. This gives an extremely sharp edge, but when you sharpen it

Above: *Traditional stag handled hunting dirks with pewter crossguards by Spanish manufacturer Muela Alcaraz; the top one has a carved boar's head pommel.*

Above: Hunting knife, believed to be of German or Austrian origin, with a jigged bone handle and a hand-made aluminum sheath.

you have to work on the whole bevel, taking care not to lose the shape of the bottom line that forms the edge.

GETTING A HANDLE ON IT

Finally we come to the handle or grip. This can be made in one piece or two. If it has two parts – sandwiching the tang – they are called "scales." The traditional materials for grips include wood, bone, antler, leather (usually as stacked and glued washers), ivory and pressed metals (steel, brass, silver plate, etc.). All of these are still used to this day, and some of them can be made to look quite spectacular and luxurious. Yet modern materials are often preferred by manufacturers, since they "do the job" and are easier to make con-

sistently and economically. Modern plastics and other manmade materials (such as ABS, G10, Micarta, Zytel, etc.) don't have some of the more unpredictable reactions to chemicals, water immersion and climatic conditions that a few of the more long-established organic materials may have. Synthetic materials are also extremely tough, and can usually be made very "grippy" with the addition of checkering, textured finishes or finger grooves, and so on.

For these reasons the more modern materials tend to be used for military and other heavy-duty applications, but are increasingly

Below: This Seeman Sub sawback clip point diving knife has synthetic handle and softer ribbed grip panels – the sheath is also man-made in a blue see-through acrylic.

Below: Alan Wood's "Walker" knife, has tight twist Damascus steel for the spear point blade and uses rare Arizona desert ironwood for the handle.

being chosen for utility and personal carry knives. Even so, various types of wood, plain or fancy, are still favorites with those that like a knife with a time-honored look and feel. Antler and bone also remain popular with the traditionalists. A few companies still use leather grips on older style models, but pressed metal handles have all but disappeared for outdoor knives.

When choosing a grip, take time to consider the type of conditions it will be used in and the sort of materials it will come into contact with. Modern synthetics are tough and easy to keep clean, but in my opinion the older materials have a better look about them. If you want the best of both worlds, go for a (real) full tang knife with riveted wood, bone or antler scales, then if they ever do get damaged, they are relatively simple to replace.

THE CHOICE IS YOURS

Hopefully the information above will have helped you in choosing a fixed blade knife. If still in doubt, go for a medium sized drop point, a clip point or a utility, which are all suitable for general duties, so you won't go far wrong.

A friend of mine who works as a cook (I refuse to boost his ego with the title "chef") has an old Sabatier knife with a 10-inch long utility type flat ground blade. My friend uses it on his boat for just

Below: Bowie style sheath knife (marked Bexfield – Sheffield, England) with a leather washer handle, which has been commonly used on this type of knife for over 100 years.

about every cutting task that a sport fisherman might encounter. These tasks range from cutting ropes to filleting fish.

When at sea this Sabatier knife hangs on a nail in the semi-covered wheel house, almost permanently exposed to the elements. The knife has a cracked wooden handle and its discolored blade is carbon steel – which is singularly unsuitable for use around salt water.

My friend, however, just swipes it across a steel before use, and it will slice through virtually anything. The only 'tender loving care' this Sabatier knife gets is a wipe over with cooking oil on a rag and then being stowed in a dry locker when the boat is moored up.

Despite the ugly appearance of this Sabatier knife it does the job required of it and my friend would never part with it – even though I have volunteered to throw it over the side of the side of my friend's boat many times….

The thing is, if you end up with a knife that will do its job half as well, it will also no doubt become a treasured personal possession, no matter what design it follows, what it is called or even what it looks like.

Below: A Condor utility/skinner with wooden grips, metal bolster and pommel. This knife is made in the United States. The knife's wide grooves on the back of the guard and the deep choil give good position and purchase for the thumb and forefinger, which in turn give better control for fine cutting.

Folding Knives

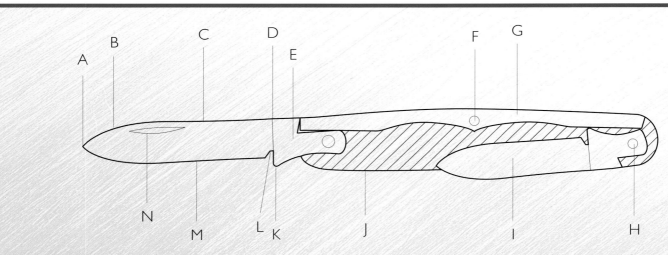

The Slip-Joint Knife

KEY
A. Blade point
B. Swedge – an unsharpened bevel
C. Back or spine
D. Shoulder – where the beveled blade meets the unbeveled tang
E. Tang – the unbeveled part of the knife that forms the joint (via an axis pin) to the handle

F. Spring pivot pin
G. Back spring
H. Blade axis pin
I. Blade (in closed position)
J. Frame
K. Kick – a part of the tang that protects the blade from touching the back spring when at rest
L. Choil – small nick in the edge of the blade just before the sharpened edge
M. Blade edge
N. Nail mark – indentation in blade to aid opening

WE KNOW THAT folding knives have been around at least since the latter part of the Roman Empire. Knives from the 2nd to the 4th centuries AD have been recovered by archaeologists. This type of knife would not have had a tensioning spring to keep it open – spring steel had yet to be invented. There would have been just a lug on the knife's spine (just behind the axis pin), that would jam against the handle when the knife was open, so it would rely on cutting pressure and/or the user's grip to keep it open.

This simplest of folding knife mechanisms has survived through the years in the form of the "penny knife," the name indicating how

Below: Penny knives were the first type of folding knives made; the illustrated knife is a 19thC Italian origin figural penny knife with boot shaped carved horn handle.

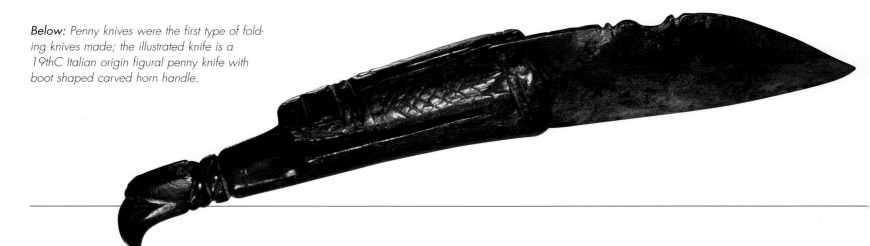

cheap these spring-less knives were in their heyday during the 18th to 19th centuries. Another indication of their low cost is that penny knives are usually very plain – unlike their ornate Roman predecessors. Although penny knives are still made in a few parts of the world, they have long been superseded by inexpensive folding knives with either a slip-joint or some kind of lock, offering a blade that doesn't require the user to exert pressure to keep it open.

SLIP-JOINT KNIVES

The slip-joint knife is sometimes called a "friction lock" even though it doesn't actually have a lock at all. Instead, there is a steel spring in the shape of a bar – called a "back spring" – which forms the spine of the handle. This spring bears against the blade's semi-circular tang (which is positioned on an axis pin) at all times, so friction offers resistance on opening the blade, while it is in use (in the open posi-

tion), and again upon closing. To open the knife you use the "nail mark," a small crescent indentation near the spine of the blade which allows a finger or thumb nail to be used to pull the blade through its axis against friction pressure from the spring. To close the knife pressure is put on the spine of the blade to swing it back through its axis until it reaches the closed position in the handle.

Many people commonly use the term "penknife" for any small slip-joint knife. Penknives were originally made for cutting and splitting quill pens in the 18th and 19th centuries, and they haven't been used for that purpose for about a hundred years. "Pocket knife" is a far better term, as this kind of knife is almost always carried in a jacket or trouser pocket. Nevertheless, the legacy of the old penknife

Below: The simple slip-joint penknife is probably the most prolific type of pocket knife in the world. This particular model is actually a two blade Swiss Army model from Victorinox.

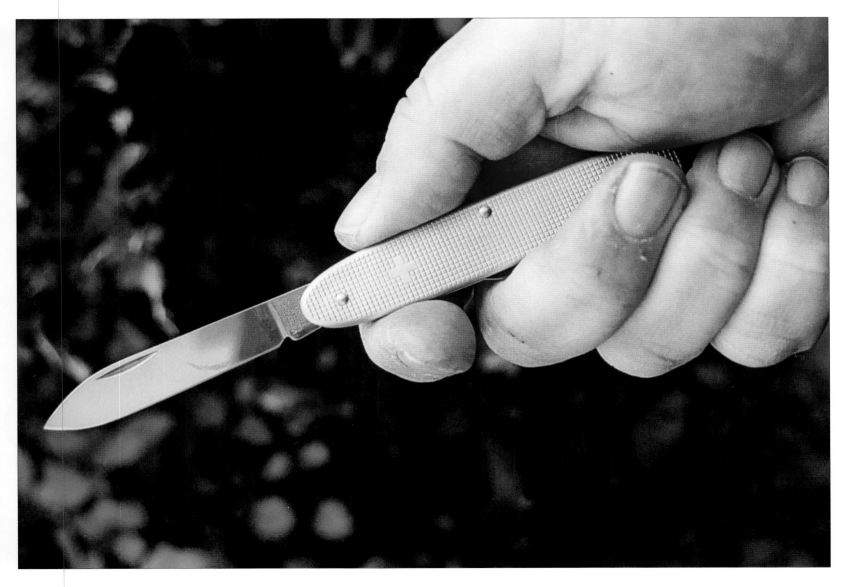

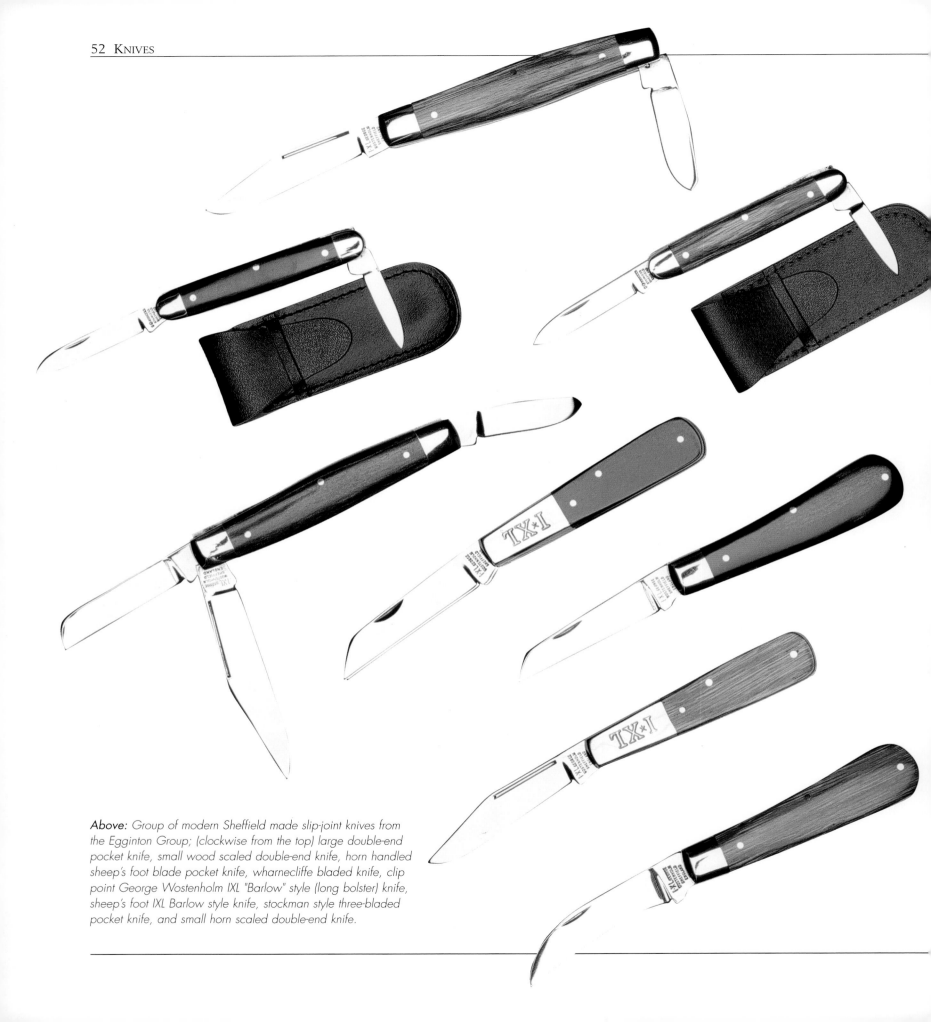

Above: Group of modern Sheffield made slip-joint knives from the Egginton Group; (clockwise from the top) large double-end pocket knife, small wood scaled double-end knife, horn handled sheep's foot blade pocket knife, wharncliffe bladed knife, clip point George Wostenholm IXL "Barlow" style (long bolster) knife, sheep's foot IXL Barlow style knife, stockman style three-bladed pocket knife, and small horn scaled double-end knife.

is retained in the "pen blade." This is a small blade with straight, unsharpened parallel spine and single edge, with an even point formed by a curve from the edge meeting a convex swedge from the spine – it is like a miniature spearpoint. This blade pattern is one of the most popular and is used in hundreds of different pocket knives, as is the slip-joint formula.

ONE, TWO, THREE OR MORE

In the "Golden Age" of Sheffield knives in the latter half of the 19th century there were thousands of different types of slip-joint pen or pocket knife designs, the great majority of which have now disappeared, to be replaced by a growing number of locking folders. But there are still plenty of these older style knives to choose from, and many of them are superbly crafted.

The first pocket knives have been around for centuries and many of them had just one blade. One famous version was the "Barlow," usually a cheap single-bladed knife with a long bolster for extra

strength, which was very popular in the 18th and 19th centuries. It was also made in a two-blade version, both blades being mounted on the same axis pin, so it is grouped in with other single-axis pin designs as a "single-end" knife. Originally made by Sheffield cutler Obadiah Barlow, this pattern became very fashionable and production was taken up by other manufacturers. Any pocket knife with a long bolster became known as a Barlow. Large versions (approximately 5in blade) were sometimes called Daddy Barlows; medium length models (approximately 3.5in blade) were Standard Barlows; and the smallest models (approximately 2in blade) were known as Baby Barlows. Sheffield-made Barlows are still available today, but there are far more European and American single-end knives to choose from.

The "Sodbuster" is a single-end pocket knife, made famous in America but with its origins in Germany. It is a strong, simple, one-blade knife, originally used by farmers, and it can be recognized by its unbolstered handle – you can see the axis pin.

The "Trapper" is a one- or two-bladed, single-end knife, made

Right: Folding knife designs like these have been around for years. These particular classics were made by Camillus – (top to bottom) two blade double-end penknife with pearl effect handles, Barlow style pocket knife and CAMCO multi-blade Camp Knife.

Below: A single-end clip point knife, another very common design; this particular knife is by Case & Sons, and bears their "XX" trademark.

Right: A 19thC twin-bladed Barlow knife from Southern & Richardson, Sheffield. The clip point blade is marked THE FARM KNIFE and there is also a spey (castrating) blade in the closed position. The long bolster of the Barlow style was meant to give extra strength and rigidity to a folding knife.

Right: A folding knife and fork combination set c1750, marked "TOOMER" on the fork. These folding combinations or separate folding knife and fork sets were once common personal possessions, especially for those who did a lot of traveling.

extremely popular in the pre-Second World War years for general outdoor work. The single-blade versions usually have a clip or Turkish clip (a longer, slimmer clip blade), with the addition of a spey blade on the two-blade models. The "Hunter" is a similar pattern but the clip blade is often accompanied by a thin "utility" type blade instead of a spey.

In order to cram even more blades into their knives (the term "blades" also includes other tools), cutlers put an axis pin at both ends of the knife, with a back spring that was pinned to the center of the handle. These are called "double-end" knives. This spring position allowed pressure to be exerted on both ends of the knife at the same time. Early models carried just a single blade on each axis pin, and these have remained one of the most popular combinations to this present day. One of the most famous of these is the "Muskrat"

GEORGE WASHINGTON'S PENKNIFE

There are many different versions of this story, but they all follow the same theme. Apparently, at Valley Forge in the winter of 1777, George Washington had a penknife (said to be a Barlow by some, but claimed to be a much fancier knife by others). It was a present from his mother when he was a teenager, given him as a reward for obeying her order not to join the British Navy as a midshipman. Apparently he carried it all his life, along with her command, "Always obey your superiors," which may sound a bit submissive now. Yet when he was about to resign his command, due to the apathy of Congress who had failed to supply his troops with proper equipment and rations, he was reminded by his colleague and friend, Major General Henry Knox, of his knife and his mother's words. So as he was still under the orders of Congress, he tore up his resignation and went on to lead his army and his country to victory.

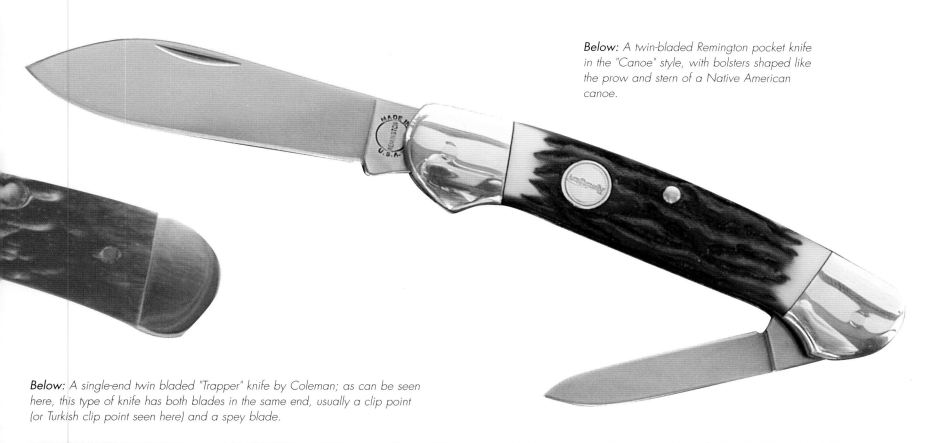

Below: A twin-bladed Remington pocket knife in the "Canoe" style, with bolsters shaped like the prow and stern of a Native American canoe.

Below: A single-end twin bladed "Trapper" knife by Coleman; as can be seen here, this type of knife has both blades in the same end, usually a clip point (or Turkish clip point seen here) and a spey blade.

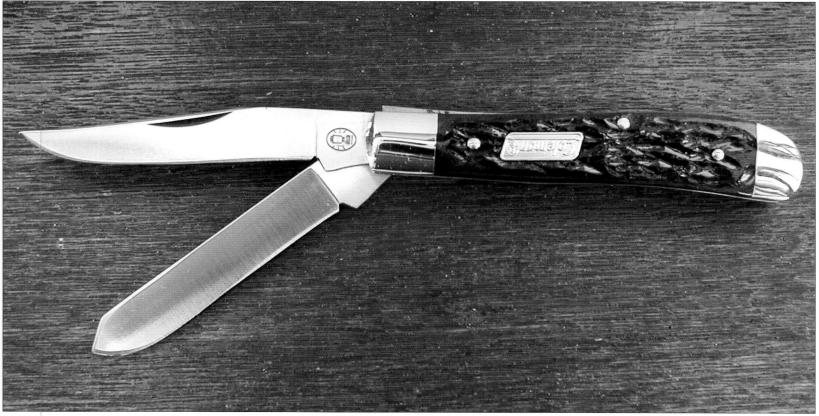

Above: This double-end Coleman knife has five blades, and there have been even larger models by other manufacturers; President Lincoln was said to carry an old eight blade pattern knife known as a "Congress."

style, a long, slim pocket knife, often with an identical Turkish clip blade at each end. "Moose" pattern knives are heavier than the Muskrat, and usually have a clip blade at one end and a spey at the other. The "Texas Jack" was a popular model a hundred years ago, but it can still be encountered, and is distinguished from other models by having a large clip blade at one end and a spear point at the other. An "Equal End Jack" looks the same at both ends when closed. One of the most famous double-enders is the "Canoe" type, an elegantly designed equal-end knife that – as the name suggests –has the look of a Native American canoe when closed, because of the curved

frame and prow shaped bolsters. Double-end knives have also been made with three or more blades. On a three-blade "Whittler" type knife, two back springs are used. Each bears on one or other of the smallest blades at one end of the knife, while they both bear on the largest blade at the other end. By the way, Whittler is just a convenient term for this type of small knife, rather than as a description of what it is actually used for – it can be used for whittling, but it also makes a nice general-purpose pocket knife. The larger "Stockman" is another classic three-blade knife, recognizable for its serpentine frame (an elongated S shape); it is a pattern that has been made by virtually every major knife manufacturer. The blades are usually a large clip alongside a smaller sheepsfoot at one end, and a spey at the other, making for a versatile knife. More tools are sometimes added, such as a sawblade, leather-punch or an awl, to make it an even more useful piece of kit. I have never seen a Stockman style knife with more than six blades, although I have heard of them, and the three- or four-blade version is much more common.

The most difficult of the slip-joint knives to make is termed a

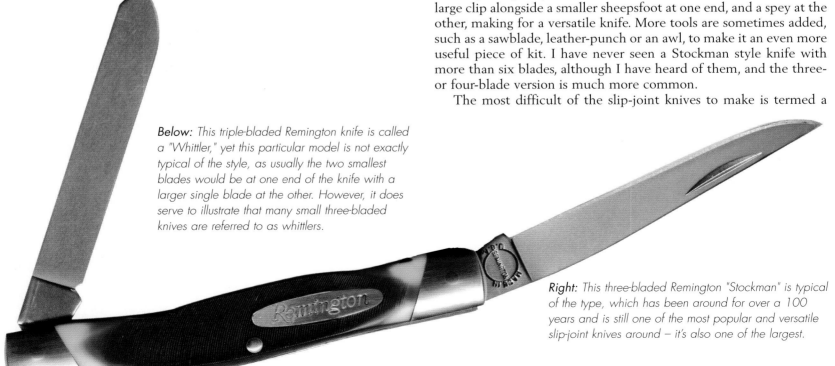

Below: This triple-bladed Remington knife is called a "Whittler," yet this particular model is not exactly typical of the style, as usually the two smallest blades would be at one end of the knife with a larger single blade at the other. However, it does serve to illustrate that many small three-bladed knives are referred to as whittlers.

Right: This three-bladed Remington "Stockman" is typical of the type, which has been around for over a 100 years and is still one of the most popular and versatile slip-joint knives around – it's also one of the largest.

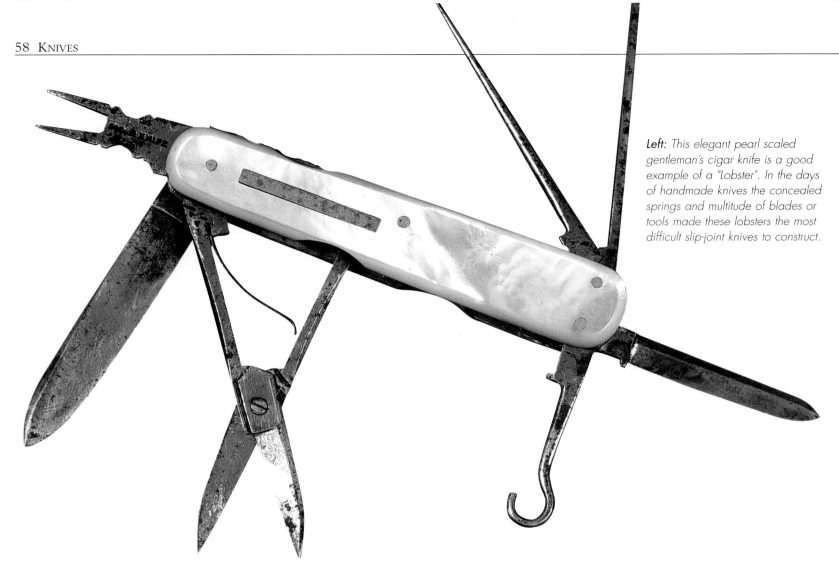

Left: This elegant pearl scaled gentleman's cigar knife is a good example of a "Lobster". In the days of handmade knives the concealed springs and multitude of blades or tools made these lobsters the most difficult slip-joint knives to construct.

"Lobster" in the trade, but they are not made exclusively for eating seafood! In fact the name is rarely used commercially, even though many of them are made – many Swiss Army knives are "Lobsters." All the term means is a slip-joint knife that has some of its springs concealed within the handle and blades on each side (instead of, or additional to, blades at either end). The blades coming out from both sides are reminiscent of the claws of a lobster – hence the name

WHY A SLIP-JOINT KNIFE?

The beauty of slip-joint pen or pocket knives is that the more delicate ones can be used for fine work yet are small enough to go in a waistcoat (vest) pocket or even on the end of a key-ring, while the larger ones are capable of tackling many cutting tasks, yet can still be comfortably carried in a trouser or jacket pocket. I have been told by British knife expert Colin Pearce that a slip-joint shepherd's knife called the "Etterick" was actually shaped so as not to excessively wear the inside of pockets.

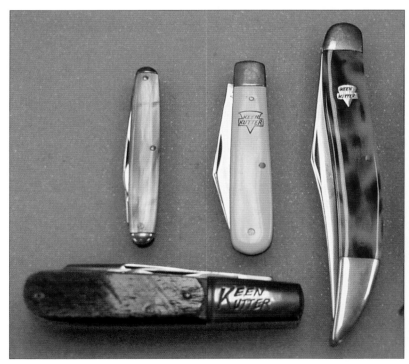

Right: More classic pocket knife designs from Camillus, an American cutlery company with roots going back to 1876. (Clockwise) Senator Penknife, One Blade Jack, Toothpick and a Keen Kutter Camp Knife.

Folding Lock-Knife Operation

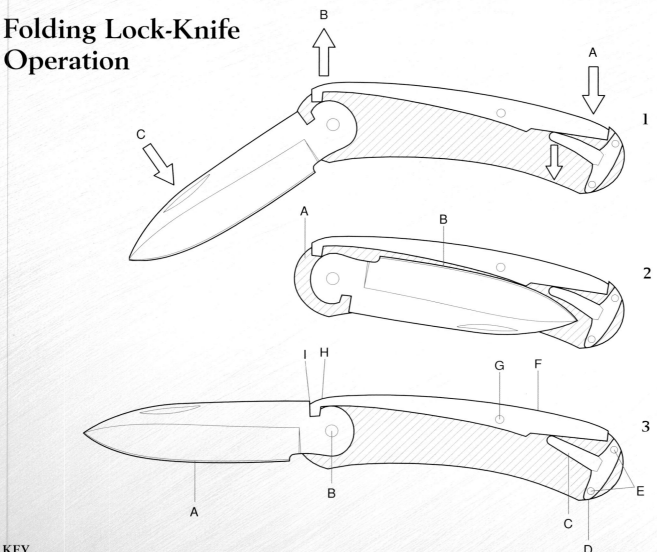

KEY

1 Blade being closed
A. Pressure is applied to the rocker-bar to depress the lock spring.
B. This lifts the locking pawl out of the notch in the tang and releases the blade.
C. The blade can now be closed, but the spring keeps a slight pressure on the tang during the closing movement.

2 Blade closed
A. Note that the lock spring keeps pressure on the rocker-bar which in turn presses the locking lug against the tang to stop the knife from swinging open accidentally.
B. The profile of the rocker-bar ensures that when the blade is closed the edge does not touch it.

3 Blade in open position
A. Blade edge
B. Blade pivot
C. Lock spring
D. Spring holding plate
E. Rivets
F. Rocker-bar
G. Rocker–bar pivot
H. Locking pawl (or lug) on end of rocker-bar
I. Notch cut out in tang for locking pawl engagement.

LOCKING KNIVES

This section deals with manually opening lock-knives. Mechanically assisted opening, gravity-operated or spring-loaded knives, usually designated as "auto-openers," "switch-blades" or "flick-knives," are dealt with elsewhere; in several states and countries they are subject to laws that are different from those that apply to a standard folder.

The most adaptable and popular outdoor knives are without doubt the various locking types. It is preferable to a slip-joint type when heavier cutting is required, or whenever a fixed blade knife is required but you can't carry one – and that latter situation occurs quite a lot in this day and age. The lock helps make such knives safer in heavy use, while their compact size makes them easier to carry and less disturbing to other citizens. Many people would consider the carrying of a fixed blade knife to be threatening and anti-social, unless seen in an outdoor work or sporting context.

Below: Many locking knives have special features to assist one handed opening, like this CRKT Ryan Model 7 which has a thumb stud on the blade. Different manufacturers employ other similar devices to achieve the same result.

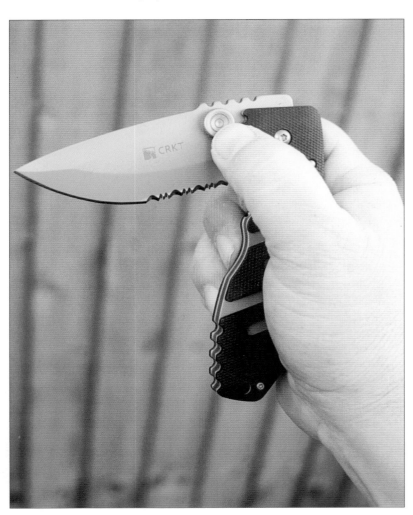

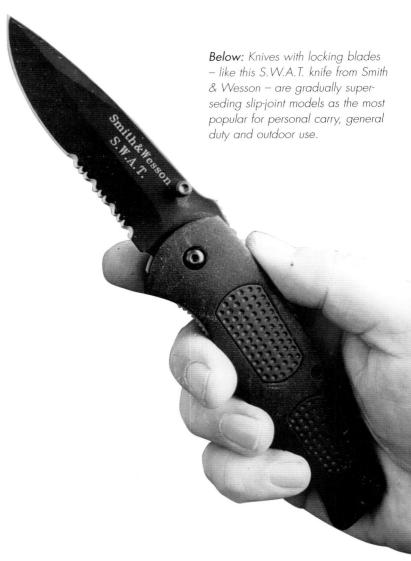

Below: Knives with locking blades – like this S.W.A.T. knife from Smith & Wesson – are gradually superseding slip-joint models as the most popular for personal carry, general duty and outdoor use.

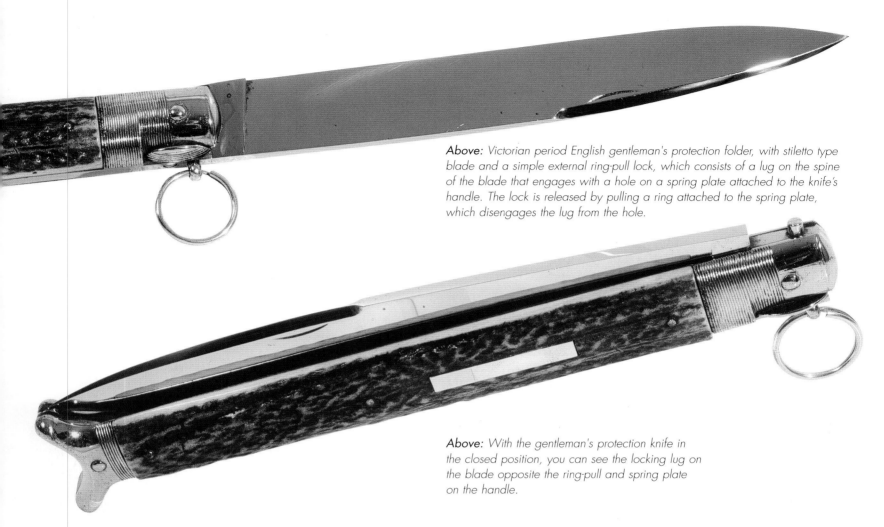

Above: Victorian period English gentleman's protection folder, with stiletto type blade and a simple external ring-pull lock, which consists of a lug on the spine of the blade that engages with a hole on a spring plate attached to the knife's handle. The lock is released by pulling a ring attached to the spring plate, which disengages the lug from the hole.

Above: With the gentleman's protection knife in the closed position, you can see the locking lug on the blade opposite the ring-pull and spring plate on the handle.

This gives the folding knife an important advantage, since its carrying length is roughly half the size of a comparable fixed blade knife. Yet it can still be used for most cutting tasks that are ordinarily encountered, including many that are normally associated with fixed blade knives. If you know what you are doing and you have a good knife with the right edge, there are few cutting tasks that cannot be accomplished with a folding knife. I have seen a Scottish poacher gralloch and field dress a fair sized red hind – including removing the head and feet – in less than five minutes, and all he used was a folding knife with a sharp, three-inch drop point blade. It may not have been the most delicate piece of field butchery but it enabled him to remove his prize from the hill unassisted.

SIZE MATTERS...

Despite this versatility, there is no doubt that in some cases size can still matter. Probably the only jobs that cannot be expected to be accomplished with a folder are high impact tasks such as heavy chopping (cutting through larger branches, or brushwood and vegetation removal). For this type of heavy outdoor work a large fixed blade or even a machete or axe would be more suitable – and a full

tang would definitely be preferred. There are also specialized cutting tasks that may require a very long blade, such as filleting very large fish or cutting large joints of meat from a carcass, in which case large fixed blade knives are more suitable.

Most locking folders tend to be between 6in and 11in or so open. This overall size comprises a handle that averages around 3.5in to 6in, which is a comfortable size for the average man's hand, and a blade that will obviously be an inch or so shorter, in order to be completely covered by the handle when it is not in use and folded away. If the handle is any longer than 6in or so, it can become unwieldy. If you have ever tried to use any of the spectacular-looking, extra large navaja folding knives from Spain, you'll know what I mean. Also it has to be remembered that a longer blade on a folding knife will put extra stress (through leverage) on the lock, hence the restriction on blade length to about 6in maximum for most folders. In Victorian times there were folding bowie knives and gentlemen's defense knives with longer blades, but in both cases they had to be carried in a sheath because a portion of the sharpened edge was left protruding, even with the knife in the folded position.

There is a clever cantilever-designed filleting knife by Paul Chen that allows a blade longer than the handle to be folded away safely,

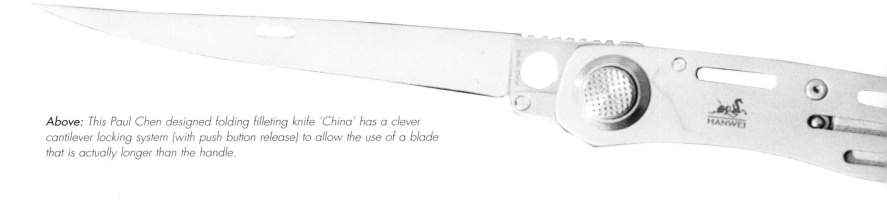

Above: This Paul Chen designed folding filleting knife 'China' has a clever cantilever locking system (with push button release) to allow the use of a blade that is actually longer than the handle.

but even this is only about 8.5in overall with a 4.5in blade. So, generally speaking, folding lock knives are limited in their length.

For an equivalent size a fixed blade will usually be stronger than a folder, although many modern locking knives will take an awful amount of abuse before they even begin to show signs of distress or mechanical failure. In fact, although I have owned many folding knives, it is only the very cheapest and poorest made that have ever let me down badly. Quality knives, even if abused, usually give you plenty of advance notice that something is about to go wrong – you rarely encounter serious and sudden lock failure. There's normally either a stiffening of the action, caused by damage or dirt, or conversely, a loosening of the blade within the handle caused by wear or slackening of the axis pin.

Provided that you start off with a reasonable quality knife, then regular inspection, along with cleaning after use and a reasonable maintenance routine, should keep it in fine fettle.

Below: The Paul Chen filleting knife in the closed position, showing part of the cantilever lock which automatically comes back to cover the extended tip of the folded blade.

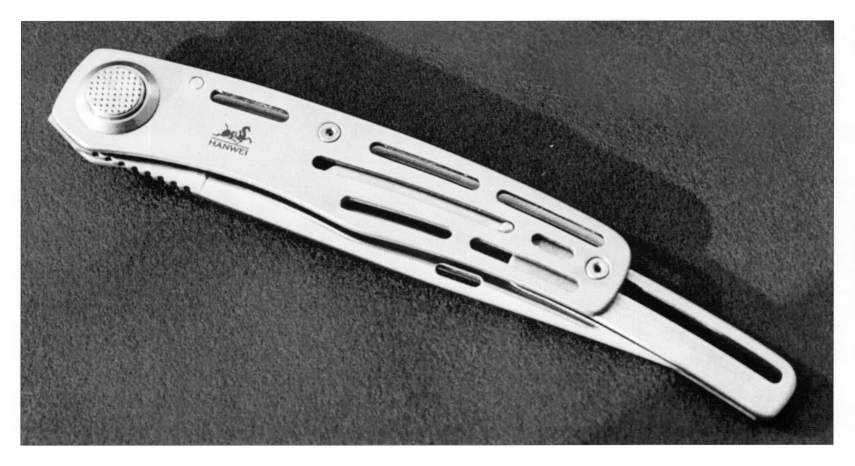

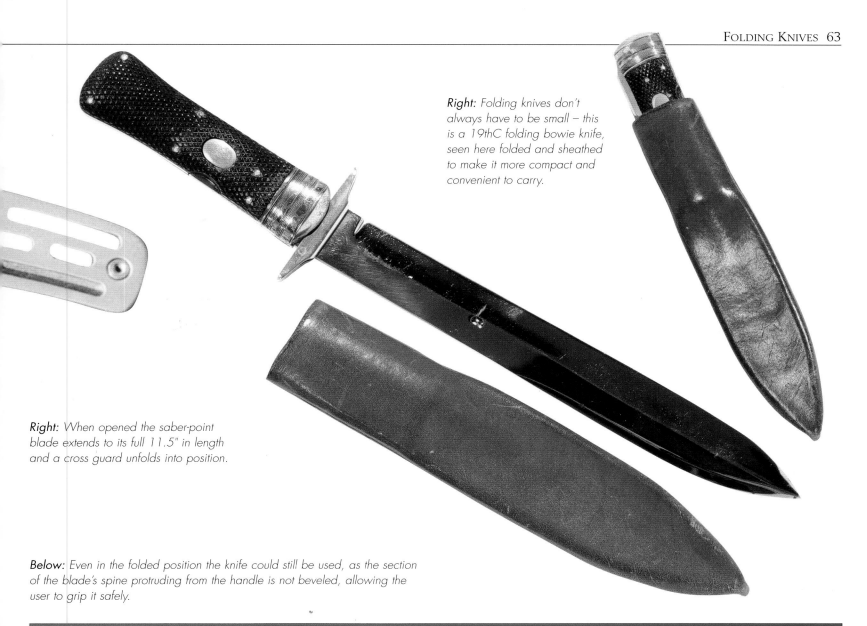

Right: Folding knives don't always have to be small – this is a 19thC folding bowie knife, seen here folded and sheathed to make it more compact and convenient to carry.

Right: When opened the saber-point blade extends to its full 11.5" in length and a cross guard unfolds into position.

Below: Even in the folded position the knife could still be used, as the section of the blade's spine protruding from the handle is not beveled, allowing the user to grip it safely.

Folding Blade Types

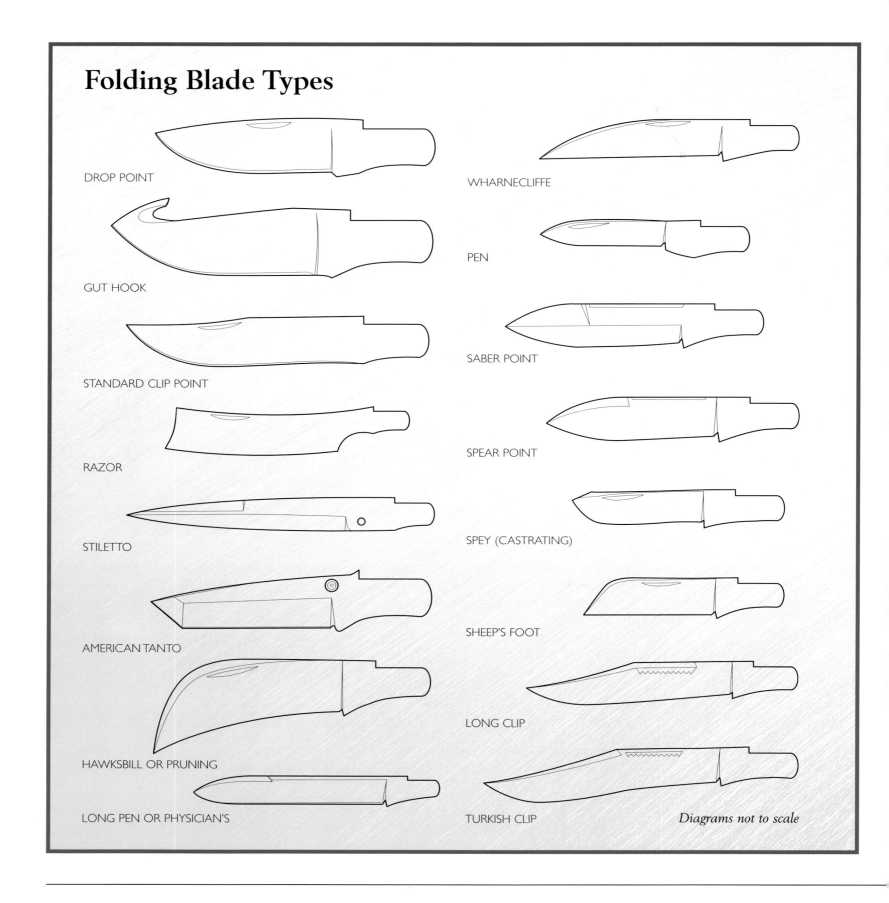

DROP POINT

GUT HOOK

STANDARD CLIP POINT

RAZOR

STILETTO

AMERICAN TANTO

HAWKSBILL OR PRUNING

LONG PEN OR PHYSICIAN'S

WHARNECLIFFE

PEN

SABER POINT

SPEAR POINT

SPEY (CASTRATING)

SHEEP'S FOOT

LONG CLIP

TURKISH CLIP

Diagrams not to scale

GETTING A HANDLE ON IT

Because of the nature of the folding mechanism, it is important that it should be as strong as possible. For this reason some folding knives are built with a type of chassis, called an inter liner, which usually consists of two slim brass or steel plates sandwiching, but not touching, the blade. The plates are joined together with screws, bolts or rivets, often passing through hollow spacer tubes so that the plates are kept clear of the opening or closing of the blade. The liners also carry the grip scales on their outer surface.

Unlike the fixed knife, the folding knife does not have a large, strong tang upon which to affix the handle. Instead, the tang is simply a short projection from the blade, big enough to form a hub to move around the axis pin that allows the knife to fold. To give the folding knife its strength at this critical point between handle and blade the locking mechanism needs to be sturdy, as does the actual handle and handle frame or inter liner that it is fixed to.

Folder handles can be made in one piece – as seen in the simple wooden knives from Opinel and other French manufacturers – but composite handles comprising two scales, with or without an inter liner, are much more common.

Handle (or haft) material for folding knives can vary widely. For grip scales, all the traditional materials (as mentioned in the fixed blade chapter) are used, along with quite a few others, ranging from fine organic choices, like mother of pearl for inlaying on some of the more delicate designs, to extremely tough, man-made materials like G-10, Micarta or Kraton, for combat or survival knives. These scales can be pinned, screwed, glued or otherwise bonded to the metal inter liner. On some designs (such as the classic back lock knife, the Buck 110) there will be a metal bolster at both ends of the handle, or just on the blade axis end of the knife. These bolsters add extra strength to the handle, particularly at the points of maximum stress.

Some knives don't have a liner lock system at all. Instead, they

Above: This wooden handled Opinel is a clasp knife, in that it has no springs to lock it, just a simple metal collar that is manually turned to block the blade from being closed. Opinel also make a similar knife but without a locking collar – so it would be classed as a "penny knife".

Below: The Buck 110 is a classic design amongst pocket knives, with a back lock mechanism, clip point blade, and a steel inter liner under hardwood scales with brass bolsters. It spawned a host of similar knives from other manufacturers and is still a popular model.

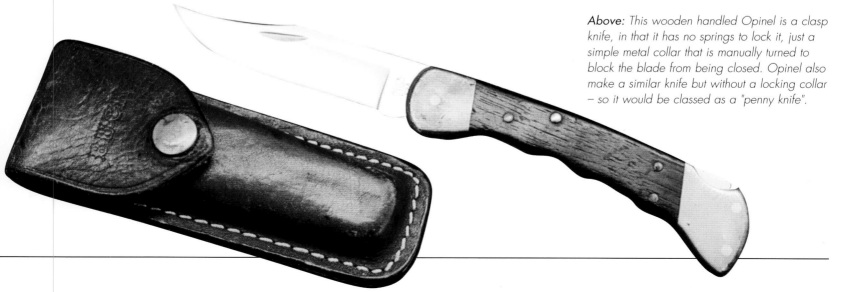

Right: The CRKT K.I.S.S. folder doesn't have separate grip scales; instead it has an all metal chassis that acts as the handle and also incorporates the locking mechanism (top). When folded the blade isn't concealed in the handle; instead it lays flush against the steel chassis (center). A full length contoured spring belt clip also helps make the K.I.S.S more substantial to grip (bottom).

rely on the integral strength of the grip scale material. Therefore, the handles for this type of knife are almost exclusively made of metal (as in the Chris Reeve titanium-scaled Sebenza or the steel CRKT K.I.S.S.), or one of the tougher, more rigid, man-made plastics (as used on the Cold Steel Land & Sea Rescue).

As with blade types, your choice of handle and grip scale material should be based on the type of use the knife will be getting, so you would think that everybody would choose one of the robust, near bomb-proof plastics. But in truth, most of us are just as likely to select a knife with a handle that we simply "like the look of." For this reason knifemakers continue to churn out fancy grip scales in shell, antler, jigged bone, exotic woods, horn, even engraved mammoth tusk. The thinking must be that, just like elaborate fishing lures, they are much more likely to catch fisherman than fish – and I should know, having been hooked and landed more than once.

KNIFE LOCKS

The following locking mechanisms are the most commonly encountered. There are many other "one-off" locks that are used by various companies or designers, but in the main they are just variations of the lock types that you will find here.

THE BACK LOCK OR ROCKER-BAR LOCK
When closed, and while being opened, the back lock acts in a similar way to a slip-joint. Both hold the blade closed within the handle

Below: This Ibberson folder has a full length back lock mechanism, the release is just above the rear bolster – the similarities with the Buck 110 are clear to see.

Left: A mid-position rocker-bar lock, seen here half way along the handle of this CRKT Cascade, is just a shorter variation of the back lock.

Above: The Buck Select is an unusual knife in that it has one blade with a slip-joint mechanism and one blade with a back lock

the case with some Cold Steel and CRKT folders.

THE LINER LOCK

A liner lock has a strip cut into one of the two metal plates that line the knife's handle and sandwich the blade when it is in the closed position. The strip is bent inwards to form a flat spring. The blade's tang is squared flat at the bottom, unlike the back lock's tang which is round. The reason for this is that, when the blade is fully open, the liner lock's flat spring pops inwards behind the squared bottom of the tang, blocking the blade and preventing it from closing. This is an extremely strong lock format, provided that it is correctly engaged; to help this process most manufacturers cut a steep bevel in the flat bottom edge of the tang, giving the liner spring something to slide into and lock up against. This should give good surface contact between both of these two lock components, even if they eventually become worn.

To release the blade the flat spring back is pushed back (the edge is usually milled to aid this operation) away from the bottom of the tang, so that the blade is free to be swung back through its axis to the closed position. To make this operation even easier, some manufacturers incorporate a button in the scale of the handle, which disengages the liner lock when it is pressed.

Unlike the back lock knife or slip-joint knife, there is no rocker-bar or back spring to put constant pressure on the blade's tang, so the liner lock knife is incredibly smooth and easy to open. But, due to this lack of spring tension, another method has to be found to

by pressure on the straight portion of the tang, then apply friction to the curved edge of the tang as the blade is being drawn through its arc around the axis pin and into the open position. The big difference is that at the point of being fully open, the slip-joint holds the blade open by friction, but does not lock, whereas the back lock does.

The back lock has a steel rocker-bar running through the back of the knife handle, with a right angle pawl (also called a lug, latch or tooth) on the end of it, permanently putting pressure on the blade's tang. The rocker-bar has a pivot pin roughly halfway down its length, and at the opposite end to the pawl there is a spring pushing upwards against the bar.

When the blade reaches its open position the pawl on the rocker-bar drops into a matching square notch on the tang, locking the blade solidly in the open position. This holds the blade open until the user operates a release mechanism. This is usually by pressing on the rear of the rocker-bar, which then pivots on its pin, lifting the pawl out of the notch, releasing the blade and allowing it to be swung back through its axis into the closed position.

The rocker-bar on the back lock can extend the full length of the knife's handle, but sometimes it extends only halfway down – as is

Right: This close up of a liner lock shows the sprung edge of the liner locked against the tang of the blade, locking it in the open position. The cut-out in the handle gives access to unlock the blade by simply pushing the liner to one side.

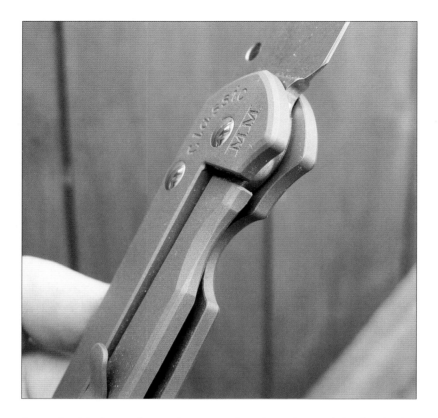

keep the blade in place when it is closed. Early models also had a back spring, so the knife was more like a slip-joint model but with a liner lock as an extra safety measure. This back spring has now been replaced almost universally with a ball détente – a small steel ball-bearing in the flat spring and a matching dimple in the tang. This keeps the blade securely stowed in the handle, but is easily overcome with thumb pressure on a stud or other opening aid at the rear of the blade (normally near the spine), allowing for a very rapid deployment of the blade with one hand.

Although the détente undoubtedly works, there is the danger of the blade opening accidentally if you drop the knife; of more concern is if the knife accidentally opens while in your pocket. To address this, some manufacturers attach a spring belt clip to the axis pin end of the knife, so that even if the détente fails, the tip of the knife will be pointing downwards, and therefore less likely to harm the user's hand when he reaches into his pocket for his knife. In spite of the potential problems, the liner lock's advantages far outweigh any disadvantages and this is now one of the most popular types of locking folder knives with both manufacturers and the users.

SEBENZA LOCK

I have heard this Chris Reeve lock described as a liner lock on steroids…. The idea is the same as the liner lock, except that the knife it is used on doesn't have an inter liner! Instead, the design uses a section of the one-eighth-inch thick titanium handle to act as the spring; as you can imagine, this lends massive strength to the lock. Two scoops of metal are removed from the locking scale to give the

Left: The liner lock on the Chris Reeve Sebenza is formed by a section of the titanium handle – this makes for a very robust lock.

lock some "spring" – enough to enable the user to be able to push the lock open. Although originally made for the Chris Reeve Sebenza folder, the lock – or copies of it – have now started to appear on other knives.

COLLAR OR RING LOCK

This is a simple locking system consisting of a split steel bolster or collar at the junction of blade and handle. The split allows the blade to pass through the collar from the closed to the open position, then the collar is turned to lock the blade in place. A slight angle on the collar allows it to be twisted tightly under the "kick" of the blade. The French Opinel knife is a good example of the ring or collar lock – without this simple ring it would be classed as a "penny knife" since it has no spring.

RING-PULL EXTERNAL LOCK

This type of lock is found on the Spanish navaja folder and a few other knives from Mediterranean, South American and African countries. The navaja's lock is in fact an external leaf spring, shaped to fit around the back of the handle and secured by pinning. It has a ring near the junction of handle and blade. The spring has a hole in the end that engages with a pin on the back of the blade's tang. To disengage the lock, the ring on the back of the leaf spring is pulled up, lifting it off the pin on the tang and allowing the blade to be closed.

BOLT ACTION LOCK

This patented lock design from Blackie Collins is used by both Gerber and Meyerco on several of their knives. When the blade is

Below: The CR Sebenza Classic 2000 has an all metal construction with a titanium handle and a S30V steel blade.

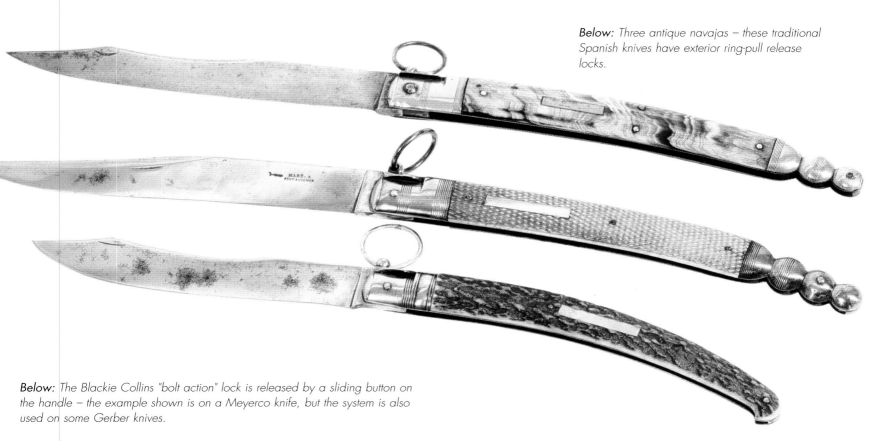

Below: Three antique navajas – these traditional Spanish knives have exterior ring-pull release locks.

Below: The Blackie Collins "bolt action" lock is released by a sliding button on the handle – the example shown is on a Meyerco knife, but the system is also used on some Gerber knives.

engage with the axis pin. This allows a shaped notch on one side of the tang to engage with a matching metal lug in the handle, locking the knife. To unlock, the blade is pushed or pulled upwards slightly – this slides the tang's slot along the axis pin and disengages the lock, allowing the blade to swing back to the closed position where another notch and pawl arrangement holds it in place.

BOKER-MATIC

This design is used on some German-made Boker knives. One of the handle scales locks the mechanism in the closed position, and has to be pushed to one side to allow a sliding button running in a slot in the handle to push the blade up through the end of the knife. At the end of the blade's travel it locks into position. To unlock the handle, the scale is once more pushed to the side and the blade slides back into the handle under spring pressure.

BALI-SONG

Also called a butterfly knife, this has a hollow handle in two parts enclosing the blade when in the closed position, with a bar latch or metal collar at the bottom to keep the two parts locked together. Each of the two handle sections is independently connected to the tang with an axis pin. To open the blade the latch is released and the handles are swung through 180 degrees to expose the blade. A fixed pin on the tang is sandwiched between the two sides of the handle for rigidity and the knife is locked open by re-engaging the bar latch at the bottom of the handles. It sounds like a long-winded operation, but a skilled user can open a bali-song in a second – often with quite a flamboyant flourish.

opened, a spring-loaded internal bolt locks the blade in place; then, to release the lock, a sliding button on the handle is operated and the blade is returned in the normal way.

NEELEYLOCK

This lock is used on some Timberlite knives, and is different from most others in that the mechanism is contained entirely in the blade axis area. From the closed position the blade is pulled slightly back (using a lug on the spine) then swung out and around as normal. But when it reaches the fully open position it drops slightly into the handle. This is because there is a slot rather than a hole in the tang to

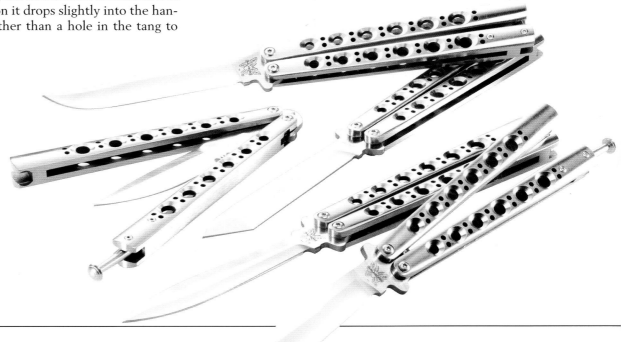

Right: The bali-song locking system – seen on these Benchmade "butterfly" knives - originated in the Philippine Islands and works by clamping the blade between the two sides of the handle. The knife has somewhat unfairly acquired a bad reputation amongst a few law authorities – even being made illegal in some countries.

Down Came a Spyder...

Although serrated edges have never really caught on for fixed blade knives, they have proved much more popular on folders. One of the chief reasons for this is the introduction of the Clipit series of knives by Spyderco around twenty years ago. This locking folder was available with a plain or serrated blade, and it soon became apparent that the serrated version offered devastating cutting ability for its size. Although this type of blade was not a Spyderco invention, their dual-height variant proved to be a very efficient and versatile edge. It would not cut as cleanly as a plain edge, nor would it be any good for skinning or other fine cutting jobs, but it would still keep cutting long after a plain edge was dull to the point of being quite useless.

The buzz-saw blade was not the only attraction. The Spyderco knife came with a humpback and a hole in the blade... yes – it really was made that way on purpose. Pretty it wasn't, but these additions made it possible to open the Clipit with one hand, and that is one huge advantage over the opposition. As a steel erector and rigger, I needed a knife all the time, but I preferred to keep at least one hand for holding on while working high above the ground. Before I owned a Clipit I had to carry a fixed blade knife in a sheath – some colleagues even carried illegal "flick knives" that weren't really suitable for heavy-duty cutting, but did give single-hand access.

The Clipit came with a steel belt clip furthermore – unsurprisingly considering the name – and this offered a much more secure carrying option. The knife could be safely clipped inside a pocket while you were climbing around, yet be easily and quickly deployed when needed. Clipit knives also sliced through rope and canvas as if they were butter.

There are now many knives available with serrated edges, one-handed opening and sprung-steel pocket clips – but most Clipit owners will always have a soft spot for that innovative, yet not so pretty, little knife.

Right: A typical Spyderco folder, with a hump on the blade spine to allow a thumbhole for easier one-handed opening, a serrated blade, and a spring clip on the handle for easy fastening to belt, waist band or pocket.

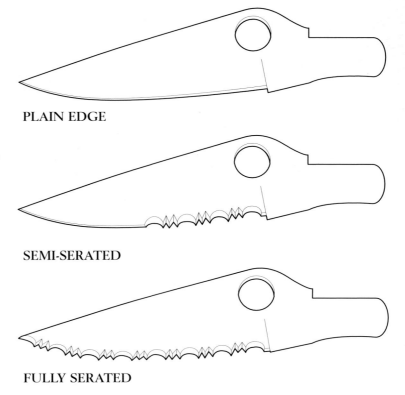

PLAIN EDGE

SEMI-SERRATED

FULLY SERRATED

Knives as Tools

ONCE KNIFEMAKERS had started to put two blades into a folding knife, it was only a matter of time before they began to incorporate secondary tools other than a cutting blade. It is likely that the first tool to be included on a folding knife was a simple spike or an awl, for piercing holes or using as a pick. In the days when the majority of people worked in agriculture, and horses were the main form of transport, a spike would have been the handiest implement to have in addition to a cutting blade. It could have been used to punch holes in leather or cloth, bore holes in wood, clean horses' hooves, open the lay of ropes for splicing, break shackle pins, align holes, relieve sheep of "bloat" and all sorts of other puncturing and leverage jobs.

As manufacturing techniques and designs improved over the years, more and more tools were added to pocket knives, sometimes on the same axis pin as the main blade, sometimes on a separate pin at the other end of the knife. In certain cases, as with some "horseman's knives" that were popular with the gentry in the mid- to late 19th century, the tools were mounted on three axis pins – the third being in the middle of the knife's spine. It was not uncommon for these knives to have five or more tools, including a cutting blade, and usually (but not always) a saw, a fleam (blood-letting tool), a hoof pick and an awl. In addition, there could be extra cutting blades, a corkscrew, leather punch, gimlet, can opener, and so on, and even removable tools such as tweezers and a tooth pick.

Other knife-and-tool combinations were developed for sportsmen and specialist trades, one of the earliest being the angler's knife, usually with a slim blade and a combination rule, scaler and disgorger, sometimes even with a miniature gaff hook. The rigger's, sailor's or yachtsman's knife is also a classic, still produced in various forms to this day. This knife normally has a sheep's foot blade, a marlin spike, and a shackle key.

Not all tool combinations were folding knives. As a Boy Scout way back in the early 1960s I can remember owning a German-made, fixed-blade bowie knife with a huge "bone" handle packed with tools. I treasured it at the time, but it was grossly top heavy and more often than not it would hang upside down from my belt.

The first practical folding knife-and-tool combination I owned was a 1950s model British Army clasp knife. It was a great outdoor tool. It featured a sheep's foot blade, combination can and bottle opener, marlin spike, and a large flat-head screwdriver protruding from the center liner plate. It was finished with black checkered plastic scales, a molded bolster, and a steel shackle. Variations on this theme dated back to before the First World War and some models are still being made today. I recently acquired a more modern model of the British Army folder made by Joseph Rodgers of Sheffield. The all stainless steel knife now has a locking blade and a more compact combination can and bottle opener, but there are no marlin spike or

Above: *The marlin spike was certainly one of the most important extra tools in the days of horse-drawn transport and sailing ships – and to the outdoorsman or yachtsman it's still a handy addition to a pocket knife.*

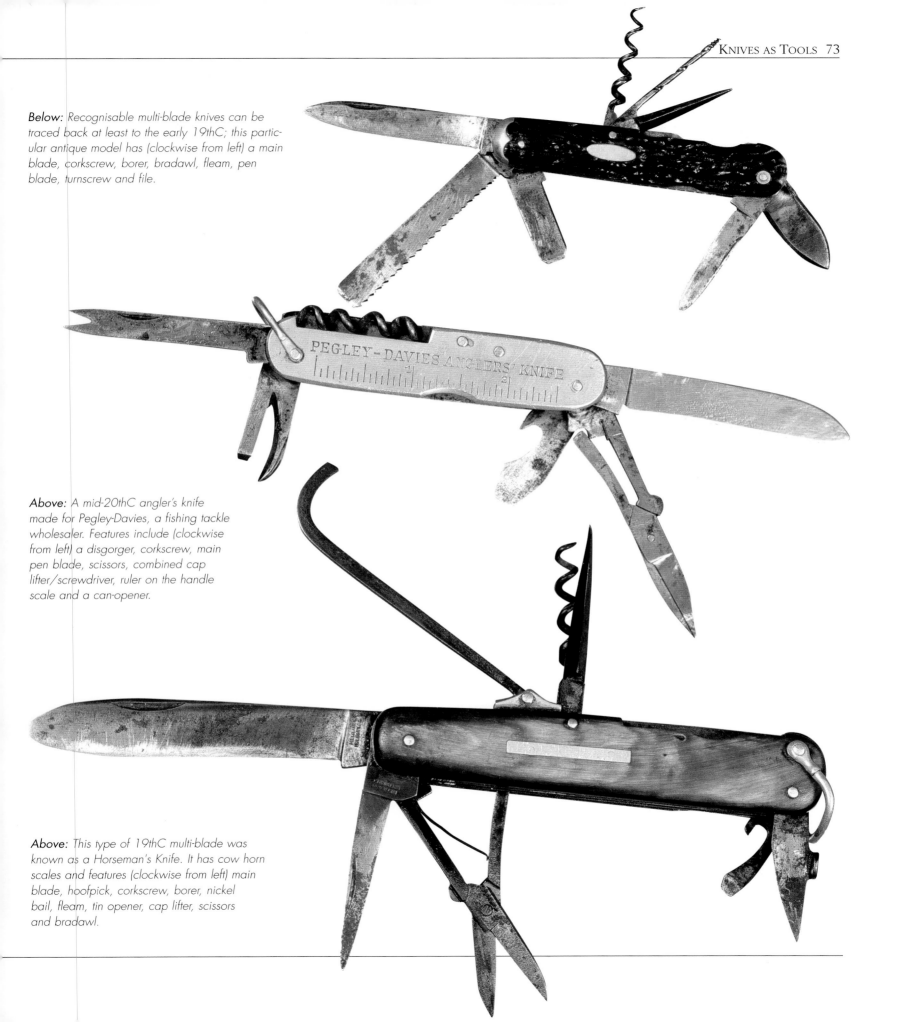

Below: Recognisable multi-blade knives can be traced back at least to the early 19thC; this particular antique model has (clockwise from left) a main blade, corkscrew, borer, bradawl, fleam, pen blade, turnscrew and file.

Above: A mid-20thC angler's knife made for Pegley-Davies, a fishing tackle wholesaler. Features include (clockwise from left) a disgorger, corkscrew, main pen blade, scissors, combined cap lifter/screwdriver, ruler on the handle scale and a can-opener.

Above: This type of 19thC multi-blade was known as a Horseman's Knife. It has cow horn scales and features (clockwise from left) main blade, hoofpick, corkscrew, borer, nickel bail, fleam, tin opener, cap lifter, scissors and bradawl.

Left: British Army jack-knife c1950s with black plastic checkered scales, slip-joint sheeps-foot blade, marlin spike, combined bottle/can opener and shackle (or bail).

Below: An original Swiss Army soldier's knife, dated 1891, with screwdriver, pen blade, bradawl and can opener.

JOSEPH RODGERS
SHEFFIELD ENGLAND
STAINLESS

Above: Modern version of the British Army jack-knife by Joseph Rodgers, Sheffield. It is of an all stainless steel construction with a locking blade.

Below: The original Swiss Army "Officer's Knife" was an improvement on the basic soldier's knife, with the addition of an extra small blade and a corkscrew.

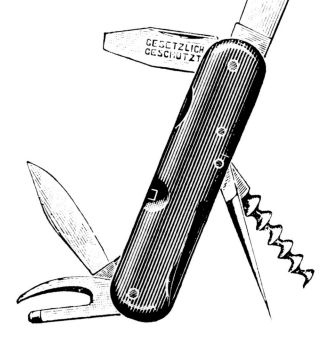

plastic grip scales. This makes for a much slimmer and lighter knife, but I would still prefer the version that retains the very useful marlin spike.

SWISS ARMY KNIVES

Perhaps the most famous of folding knife-and-tool combinations is the Swiss Army knife, which dates back to 1886 when the Swiss Army decided to equip every soldier with a regulation pocket knife. In 1889 the Army issued a new rifle, the Schmidt-Rubin, and put out a tender for a new model of multipurpose knife designed as a rifle accessory. The national arms company – the Fabrique Nationale d'Armes – turned down the work, but a Swiss cutler called Karl Elsener (whose company was to become famous as Victorinox in 1921), along with other members of the Association of Swiss Master Cutlers, began to make knives for the Army. Yet they still couldn't cope with the volume of knives required, so some of the work went to German cutlers in Solingen.

Towards the end of the century, a company called Paul Boechat & Cie, later to become Wenger, also began making Swiss Army knives under contract. In 1908 the Swiss government awarded half of the army knife contract to Elsener and half to Wenger. Both companies were also granted the right to use the Swiss cross in a shield as a trading symbol. For this reason, to this day, Wenger's claim to be the manufacturer of the "Genuine Swiss Army Knife" and Victorinox's counterclaim to produce the "Original Swiss Army Knife" are both valid.

Below: Modern version of the Swiss Army "Officer's Knife" by Wenger has all the functions of the original, plus a few other creature comforts.

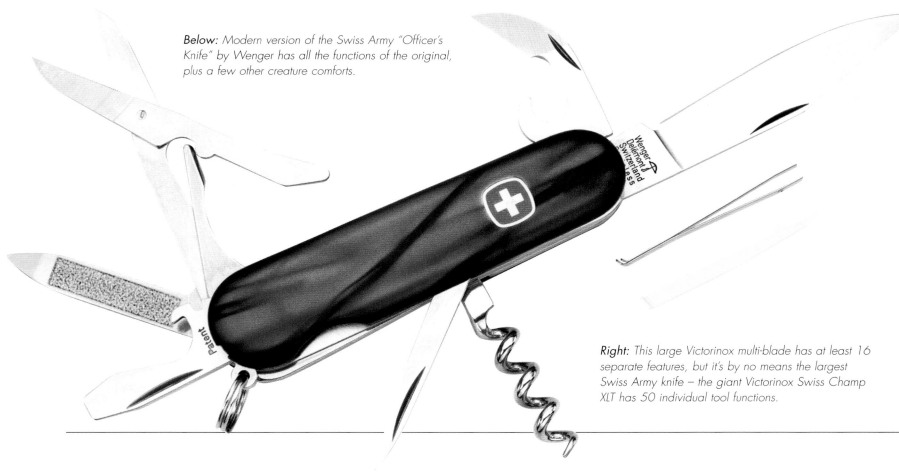

Right: This large Victorinox multi-blade has at least 16 separate features, but it's by no means the largest Swiss Army knife – the giant Victorinox Swiss Champ XLT has 50 individual tool functions.

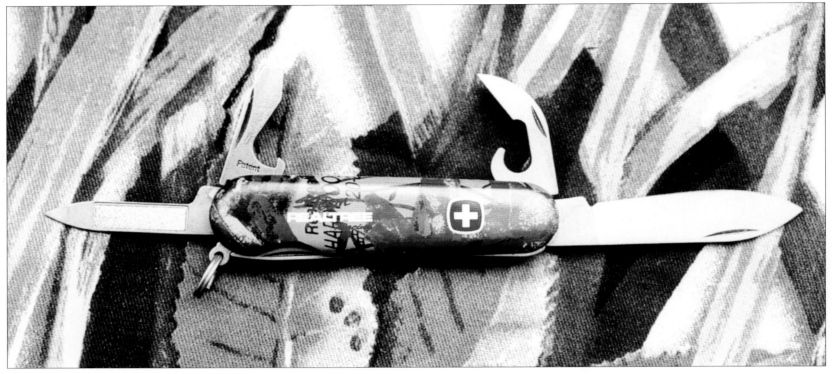

The original soldier's knife design incorporated a cutting blade, reamer or awl, screwdriver and can opener. Elsener developed a lighter model, the "Officer's Knife," that had all the implements of the soldier's model, plus a small secondary blade and a corkscrew. It is this last model, and derivatives thereof, that have become famous world-wide as the Swiss Army knife.

Today, the Victorinox and the Wenger ranges offer dozens of different combinations, from small knives with four or five tools to large knives with over a dozen different utensils.

THEN CAME THE MULTI-TOOLS

The original multi-tool was the Leatherman, and it was totally different from the Swiss Army style pocket knives that had come before. Instead, it was based on a set of folding pliers as the primary tool with a useful selection of fold-away secondary implements built into the U-section steel handles.

Equipment reviewers in outdoor magazines raved about this new

Above: Swiss Army knives certainly move with the times; this Wenger knife has modern Realtree camouflage scales and satin finish blades.

Right: The Leatherman was the first of the pliers-based multi-tools that started a mini revolution in pocket knives – this particular model is the Supertool 200. (Photo by John Fenna)

"wonder tool," and once I had used one I had to agree with them. In truth, there were a few criticisms that could be made, but the advantages far outweighed these. The Leatherman sold like hot cakes and other cutlery companies jumped on the bandwagon of the pliers-based multi-tool, some of them adding significant improvements over the original, while some others did not! Unfortunately, the success of good quality multi-tools has also led to lots of cheaper variations, but this is one area where you really do get what you pay for... a cheap tool is almost always a useless tool. The trouble is, you don't usually find out until you really need it to work well, and it fails you.

To my mind the multi-tool is useful in situations when you haven't got access to your normal toolkit. This doesn't necessarily mean that it's only good for emergency situations, since there are plenty of people who use a multi-tool for everyday tasks. I just think that the individual secondary implements on the pliers chassis are at best a good "make-do" when you haven't got a purpose-built separate tool for the job. For instance, anybody who has used a screw-driving utensil on a multi-tool (or pocket knife for that matter) will tell you that an ordinary screwdriver will do the job far easier. Likewise, if you find that you use the knife blade on your multi-tool everyday, surely it would be easier to carry a separate knife as well as the multi-tool.

In my opinion the big advantage of most "multi" models is that they are built around a set of pliers, a primary tool that I find extremely useful. Other people will tell you that the pliers are not as important as the other functions, to which I would say, "If you want tools but don't need pliers, then buy a Swiss Army knife."

BEST BITS

When choosing a multi-tool it is best to decide on all the tasks and scenarios you may need it for, then buy one that suits your criteria. I know that this sounds blindingly obvious, but you would be surprised at how many people buy models that don't have the features they really need. For sport in the great outdoors, a medium size model with traditional tools such as blade, saw, awl, etc., should suit, while a smaller model incorporating a good set of scissors might be better for an office worker. The larger, heavier sets, with the maximum amount of implements, could be the choice of the emergency

Left: As functions and materials are improved, the price of multi-tools has gone up, but models like this Smith & Wesson 44 Mag can still have plenty of functions while remaining affordable.

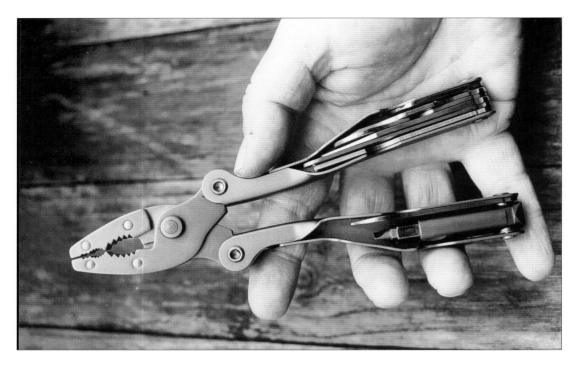

Left: The Shrade Tool has all the tools in its handles facing outwards, so they can be accessed even when the pliers function is folded away.

or a bottle cap remover, although some people would see these as essentials. Personally I see these as unnecessary extras, and if I really need to get into a bottle, I'll do it with whatever tools are to hand – or no tools at all for that matter.

A number of manufacturers offer additional kits to accompany their multi-tools. These usually consist of a selection of flathead and cross-head screwdriver bits and/or sockets for bolts. These bits can be fitted to a driver shaft or adaptor on the main tool chassis, thereby increasing the capabilities of the tool. Personally, I would not want any "attachments" that could be completely detached from the main tool – I'd just lose them. There are people who would disagree with me on the issue of attachments, probably arguing that if you

services or heavy industry worker. Whatever your needs, there should be a model to suit.

Here are my suggestions for a good, all-round multi-tool: snipe-nosed pliers with wire cutter and stripper, clip or spear point plain cutting blade, sheep's foot serrated cutting blade, a wood saw, scissors, large, medium and small flathead screwdrivers, small cross-head screwdriver, a good quality medium and fine file, an awl, a can opener, a lanyard hole and/or a strong split-ring, and finally a weather resistant belt pouch. Note that I haven't included a corkscrew

are buying a multi-tool for its potential in unexpected situations, then it is best to have as many utensils at your disposal as possible. The final choice is yours.

I know that some people carry two multi-tools, or a multi-tool and a Swiss Army type knife, to get all the features that they need. This has the advantage of giving you two separate tools for certain jobs that might require them both to be deployed. However, I recently saw a guy in a shopping mall with eight multi-tool and knife pouches slung around his waist. It looked like the man was

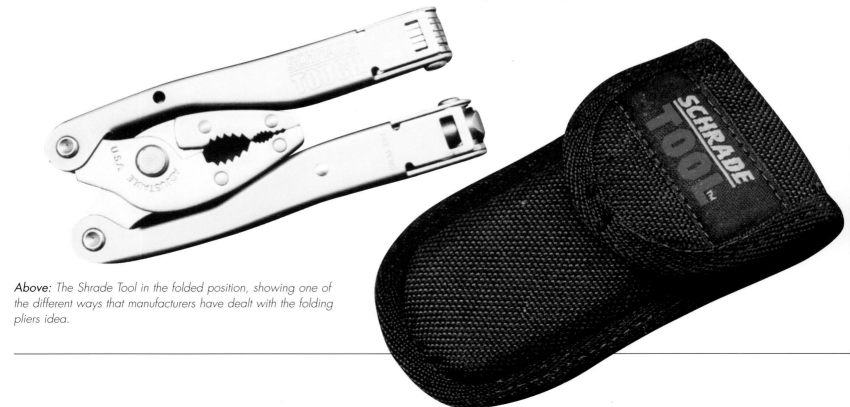

Above: The Shrade Tool in the folded position, showing one of the different ways that manufacturers have dealt with the folding pliers idea.

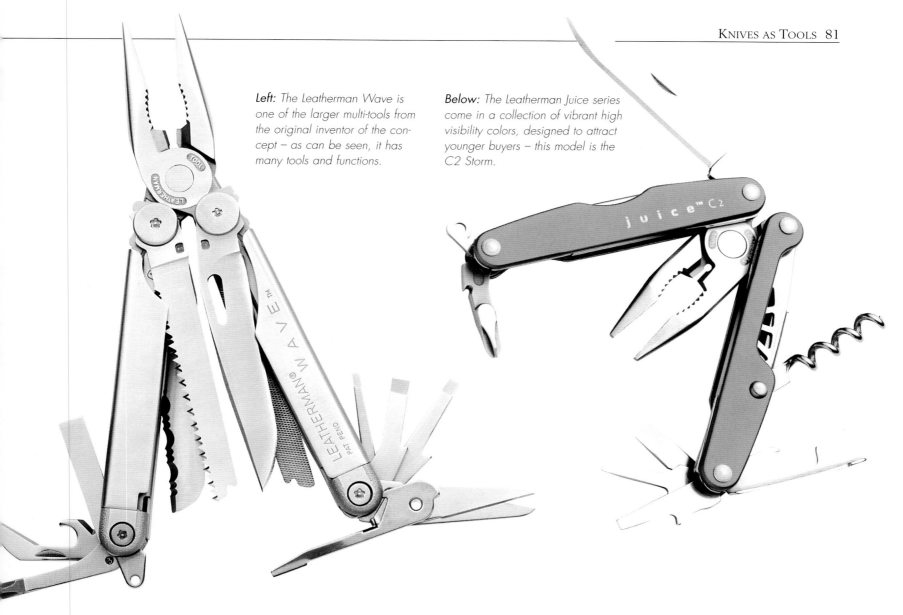

Left: The Leatherman Wave is one of the larger multi-tools from the original inventor of the concept – as can be seen, it has many tools and functions.

Below: The Leatherman Juice series come in a collection of vibrant high visibility colors, designed to attract younger buyers – this model is the C2 Storm.

wearing Batman's utility belt. This may be an extreme case, but it does reinforce my earlier point – if you are going to load yourself up with that much kit, you may as well carry a tool-roll or toolbox.

THINGS TO LOOK FOR

When choosing your multi-tool make sure that the primary tool is up to the job you want it for, because it is probably the main reason that you are buying it instead of a knife-based ensemble. In the case of pliers, make sure that they can be deployed easily and that the handle assemblies are rigid in use – if they flex too much under load they may misalign, making it difficult to deploy or return the tools that they contain.

Another important consideration is whether the tool functions are lockable or not. Many are locked by sliding catches, or by closing the handle back down after deploying the tool. There are a few models where it is impossible to lock the tools, and in my opinion this is a big turn-off.

One of the best multi-tools is made by the originators of the

genre – Leatherman. The "Wave" model is a great improvement on previous Leatherman tools, being easier to deploy than the original and with tools that can be used without opening the pliers. Leatherman have also introduced their colorful, compact and affordable "Juice" range, each model coming with a different set of features designed to appeal to the younger sports user.

The Gerber company are probably the most prolific makers of

Below: Another model from Leatherman; this time it's a mini multi-tool that could be attached to a keyring. Appropriately it's called the Squirt.

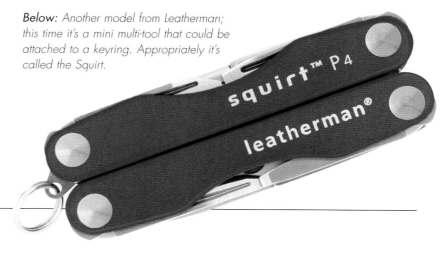

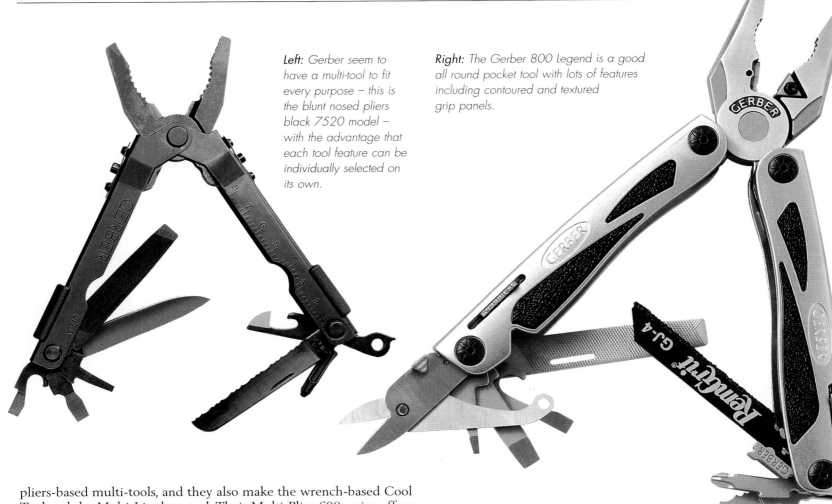

Left: Gerber seem to have a multi-tool to fit every purpose – this is the blunt nosed pliers black 7520 model – with the advantage that each tool feature can be individually selected on its own.

Right: The Gerber 800 Legend is a good all round pocket tool with lots of features including contoured and textured grip panels.

pliers-based multi-tools, and they also make the wrench-based Cool Tool and the Multi-Lite box tool. Their Multi-Plier 600 series offers eleven different models, all with one-handed opening pliers and lockable tools. The Compact Sport 400 is three-quarters the size of the 600 series, while the Gerber 650 Evolution offers interchangeable pliers heads (blunt and pin nose in early 2003, with a special fishing head and a wire cutting head introduced subsequently). The 800 Legend model has tools that can be accessed with the plier function closed, plus a RemGrit jigsaw blade attachment and a triangular tungsten insert in the wire cutting part of the pliers jaw. The 700 Urban Legend model incorporates all the knowledge that the company has accumulated with previous models but in a more compact package.

SOG now have quite a few models in their range, but their PowerLock tool is particularly interesting with its interlocking gear system that gives extra leverage – claimed to be twice the power of conventional designs. It also features covers that fold over the tool compartments to stop the edges of the handles biting into your hand when using the pliers.

The Kershaw Multi-Tool has non-folding pliers that are slightly angled and have a useful adjustable locking function. The other tools are good, can be easily accessed and lock up securely. Other models to look out for are the Schrade Tough Tool, the Bucktool, and the SpyderRench which is unusual to say the least, but then that is what we've come to expect from its maker, Spyderco.

Below: This SOG PowerLock EOD (Explosive Ordnance Disposal) model is specially designed for military applications, with compound leverage pliers, a blasting cap and demolition cord crimper.

SWISS ARMY MULTI-TOOLS

All things tend to go full circle, and the knife-making industry is no exception. Hence it should be no surprise that both Victorinox and Wenger have produced their own pliers-based multi-tools... and both companies have made a good job of it.

The Victorinox tool has everything tucked neatly away, but all the features except the pliers are accessible from the outside. The tools are precision made and lockable, yet are easily released using a positive sliding catch. All in all, a great design.

The Wenger company's offering, unimaginatively called the Pocket Grip, has half the pliers grip and jaw built into a large lock knife chassis, with the other half of the pliers hinged onto it. All the usual features are there and the whole assembly looks rock solid, but it is a bit on the large side. Once again, this is knife is a quality item.

Who knows, perhaps Swiss Army multi-tools will become as famous as Swiss Army knives?

Above: The Wenger Pocket Grip tool is actually more like a Swiss Army knife with added pliers and screwdriver attachments – yet it is still fairly compact and pocketable.

Right: The first pliers-based Victorinox multi-tool still managed to look like a giant Swiss Army knife, but although it was a very large and strong tool, it may have been too substantial, as the company have now gone for a more orthodox all steel lighter weight folding multi-tool.

Combat, Survival and Rescue Knives

W**HILE THE** knife was one of man's first tools, it was also one of his first weapons, and throughout history there has always been this dichotomy. Combat, survival and rescue knives are perfect examples of this, the first of which may be designed for the taking of life, the second for the sustaining of life, and the last for the saving of life.

Right: The stiletto dagger is a knife that is recognisably designed as a weapon only, rather than as a tool; (left to right) a diamond section English stiletto c1600, an Italian 17thC stiletto with hollow triangular blade, a small 17thC German or Italian main gauche (left hand) parrying dagger, a 17thC Italian stiletto with diamond section blade, and a slender diamond section 17thC Italian all steel stiletto. (Photo courtesy of Bonhams, London)

Below: In earlier times the type of knife one carried would give a good indication of your status – this Italian 15th century "ear'" dagger with finely engraved gold and ivory handle would have been owned by a very wealthy man.

EARLY COMBAT KNIVES

Soldiers have always carried knives, for use both as weapons and tools, but they often had to supply their own – and still do in some cases – rather than receive one as part of their kit.

From medieval times, before the formation of standing armies, wars were generally fought by a central core of professional warriors led by a king or other nobleman, and backed by a much larger force of yeomanry or a civilian militia. Although there would have been some arms available from the local armory, much of this force would have been expected to supply their own weapons – professionally made arms and armor for the knights and men-at-arms, but converted tools and possibly home-made bows for much of the force (who would almost always have been agricultural workers). The one weapon that would have been in common to all of them would have been a knife. The lords would have had expensive hand-made dirks, often sumptuously decorated; the knights and professional soldiers would have had purpose-made daggers (often with narrow blades to exploit small gaps in the enemy's armor); but the ordinary conscripted soldier would have had the same knife with which he did his work or ate his dinner!

While the king or emperor would have been quick to call on the service of commoners in times of war, and would have expected them to turn up armed and ready for battle, in peace time they would often have made it illegal for ordinary citizens to carry arms. Swords were reserved for men of rank, gentlemen or professional soldiers. Yet these were still dangerous times, so the common man would have carried a knife for protection as well as day to day chores.

Some rulers in their fear of revolution would have denied him even that....

Even so, knives continued to be carried for defense and certain design trends began to emerge. Slim-bladed, double-edged daggers, made almost exclusively as weapons, became commonplace in the Middle Ages, with designs such as the rondel, baselard and ballock knives differing mainly in the shape of their hilt. Other knives, more

Below: Close-up detail of the ear dagger's characteristic handle.

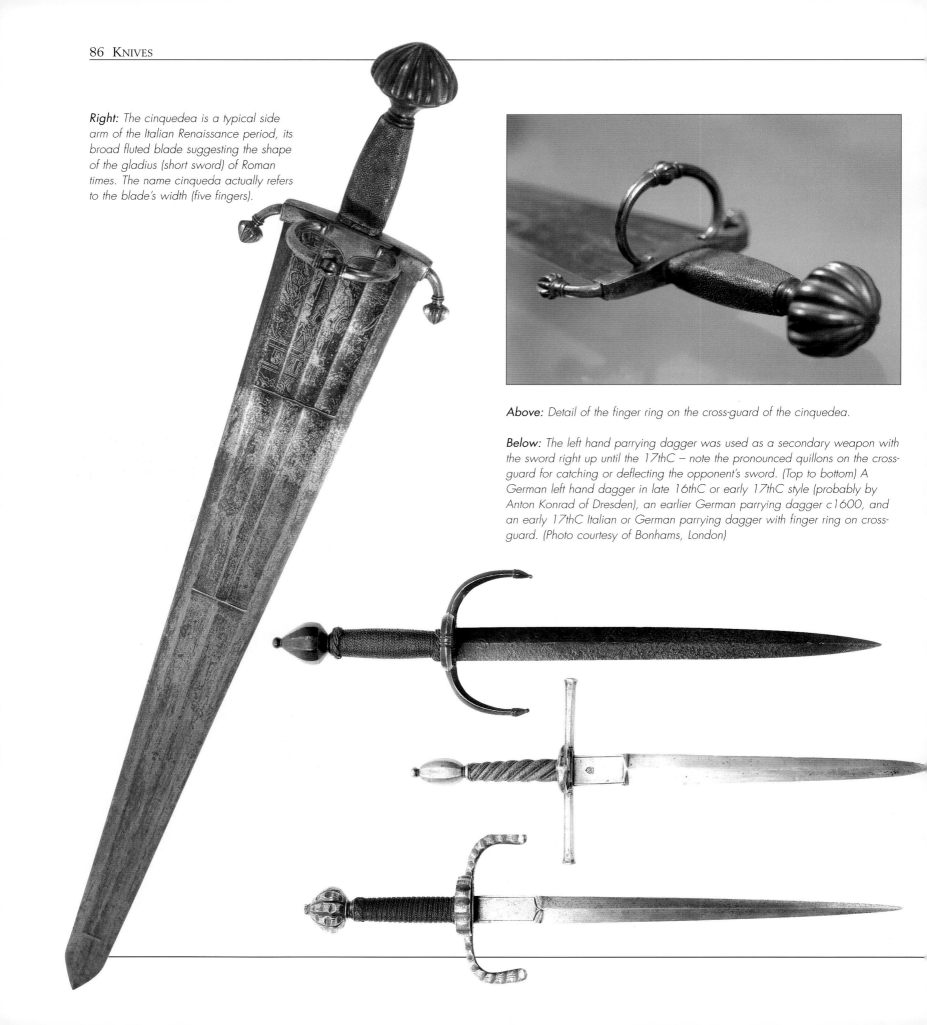

Right: The cinquedea is a typical side arm of the Italian Renaissance period, its broad fluted blade suggesting the shape of the gladius (short sword) of Roman times. The name cinqueda actually refers to the blade's width (five fingers).

Above: Detail of the finger ring on the cross-guard of the cinquedea.

Below: The left hand parrying dagger was used as a secondary weapon with the sword right up until the 17thC – note the pronounced quillons on the cross-guard for catching or deflecting the opponent's sword. (Top to bottom) A German left hand dagger in late 16thC or early 17thC style (probably by Anton Konrad of Dresden), an earlier German parrying dagger c1600, and an early 17thC Italian or German parrying dagger with finger ring on cross-guard. (Photo courtesy of Bonhams, London)

Above: Replica 18thC butcher's knife by John Nowill & Sons of Sheffield (est. 1700, now part of the Adams Group). This type of knife would have been carried and traded throughout the American frontier.

suitable for cutting than stabbing, were made with just one beveled and sharpened edge, leaving a thicker spine for greater strength. Many knives reflected the designs of swords of their particular period; they were just smaller, but in some cases the knives became so big that it was difficult to tell when they had become a sword. The 15th Century German "Grosse Messe" (big knife) was actually a short curved sword, and the Italian cinquedea – a broad-bladed, double-edged weapon – would often fall somewhere between the description of a large knife and small sword.

The period between the late 14th until the mid-17th centuries was probably the high point for design of civilian fighting knives in Europe, reflecting the interest in the use of the main gauche (left hand) dagger as a secondary weapon during sword-fighting duels, and the stiletto as a primary weapon for the assassin in the murky and devious world of Renaissance politics.

Arguably the next great leap forward in combat knives was more due to adaptation than invention, and it occurred when the explorers from the Old World met the natives of the New World. Cheap iron working knives from Europe, commonly called butcher or trade knives, were traded with the native tribes (along with other metal articles), in some cases boosting their technology from Stone Age straight into the Iron Age in just a few decades. It is hard to imagine how much of an advantage an iron blade might have had over a flint, but there's no doubt that in the early days of European colonization steel blades were highly prized by Native Americans. Some native knives became very distinctive, such as the "beaver-tail" or DAG, which had a broad steel blade apparently designed originally to be traded as a lance tip.

In the years of struggle that symbolize the birth of modern America, both frontiersmen and natives used their working knives as weapons against each other as they fought for their very survival.

It was in this harsh environment during the early part of the 19th

Below: This chipped and shaped obsidian blade would have been a good example of Native American tribal technology, until the arrival of European colonists with steel trade knives.

SCALPING AND SCALPING KNIVES

Depending on which research you believe, the Native American practice of scalping was first encouraged by the French, the Dutch or the British colonists. The taking of the scalp was to enable a poll (literally, a head-count; poll is also another name for the top of the head – where the scalp comes from) to be carried out in order that bounty to the natives could be paid for killing one's enemies. The practice was first used to incite friendly tribes against hostile "savages," but then it was extended against European enemies. Eventually, the practice spread west and the Plains tribes took scalps just for the sheer hell of it… and as a way for a warrior to exhibit his prowess by displaying the scalps of his enemies.

Sometimes references to "scalping knives" or "scalpers" occur on 18th century invoices and manifests. I have no doubt that this was the name given to knives handed out to natives for the purpose of scalping, but I doubt that this was what the knives were originally made for. Having seen a few so-called scalping knives in museums (and a couple of modern replicas), I believe that they look very much like other knives of the period variously called cook knives, camp knives, working knives, or simply trade knives. They usually have a single edge and sharp point and are narrower than any of the more common heavy "butcher" type trade knives, but in my opinion they are still just a variety of trade knife. But of course this is nowhere near as exciting, crowd-pulling or marketable a name as "scalping knife." I think that indigenous people would use any knife that was to hand, and although a design similar to a skinning or caping blade would probably have been better for the task of lifting the scalp from the skull, any sharp knife would have done the job.

Below: This replica scalping knife by John Nowill & Sons, Sheffield, is said to reproduce the pattern favored by Native Americans for use in scalping – notice how closely it resembles a modern cook's knife!

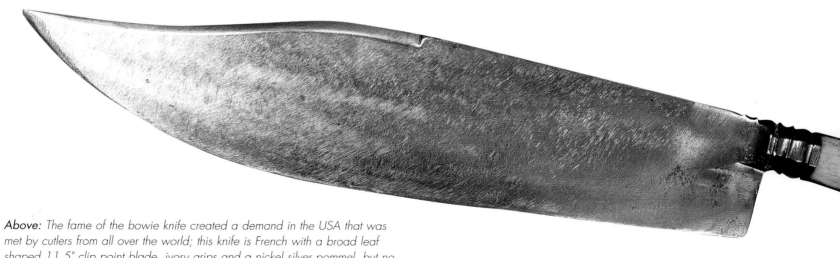

Above: The fame of the bowie knife created a demand in the USA that was met by cutlers from all over the world; this knife is French with a broad leaf shaped 11.5" clip point blade, ivory grips and a nickel silver pommel, but no quillons (the drop blade shape negates the need for a guard).

Left: This British trench dagger of First World War has a brass knuckleduster handle. This looks like quite a handy weapon, but this picture shows the only possible hand-hold (the position and size of the finger holes make it impossible for most people to hold it in a blade up position) which means that despite its looks it's not a very versatile fighting knife.

century that one of the most famous fighting knives emerged. This was of course the bowie knife, as carried by James Bowie. Much has been written about this knife, and there is a great deal of controversy surrounding it. The knife receives closer attention elsewhere in this book; suffice to say here that the format of a medium to large knife with a single edge and a clip point blade has become one of the most famous designs for a fighting knife – a truly legendary weapon and tool that has been adopted for both civilian and military use. The only design that comes anywhere close to its popularity as a basis for a fighting knife is the twin edged, spear or saber point, dagger – and some would claim that to be the "original" bowie design, but more of that later.

20TH CENTURY COMBAT KNIVES

We will take the early part of the 20th century as a starting point for considering military combat knives, simply because you are more likely to encounter army issued knives made specifically for hand-to-hand combat from this point on. Before this the main "issued" edged weapon to the common soldier was a bayonet – and these will be dealt with in a later chapter. Other types of knives were also issued

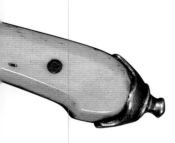

Right: Four bowie knives showing different styles and handle materials; (left to right) a conventional clip point blade with stag antler handle, a spear point blade with ivory grips, another spear point blade this time with a gutta percha (a rubber material) covered handle, and finally a fancy clip point bowie with decorated metal cross-guard and pommel with horn scales.

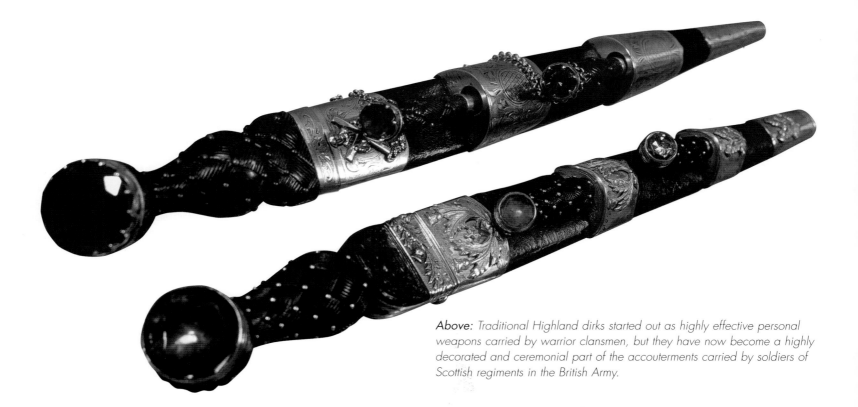

Above: Traditional Highland dirks started out as highly effective personal weapons carried by warrior clansmen, but they have now become a highly decorated and ceremonial part of the accouterments carried by soldiers of Scottish regiments in the British Army.

to ordinary soldiers, but these were as general tools – the Swiss Army knife is a perfect example. Officers, noncommissioned officers and the like may have been issued with swords and even ceremonial dirks, but they don't fall within the definition of a combat knife for our purposes.

It was the First World War, with its stalemate tactics and consequent trench raiding, that encouraged the development of special edged weapons to gain an advantage in hand-to-hand fighting. In a genteel Edwardian age following on from the even more constrained Victorians, British cutlery designers nevertheless devised some of the most wickedly vicious edged weapons that you will ever see. The strange thing is that there is no record of trench knives being generally issued to British troops. Instead, they had to make or buy their own. Luckily there were plenty of daggers and knuckleduster knives available privately from Sheffield cutlers such as George Ibberson,

Hibbert & Sons, and William Rodgers. A company called Robbins of Dudley also made dagger-type trench knives, knuckleduster knives and some particularly nasty push daggers – some with edged blades and others with spikes (like an ice-pick but with a T-bar handle and knuckle guard). The French had a knuckle bowed spike called the Clou Francais (the French Nail), while the American "doughboys" had the M1918 fighting knife, complete with brass knuckleduster, dagger blade and "skull crusher" steel pommel. I understand that modern replicas of this last knife are available.

More of the same styles were available for private purchase in the Second World War, because even though trench warfare was a thing of the past, close quarters combat still occurred. However, by this time more combat/utility fixed blade knives were being officially issued to troops.

In the USA several manufacturers developed fighting knives, and

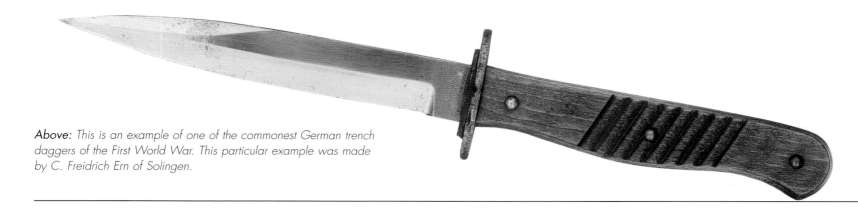

Above: This is an example of one of the commonest German trench daggers of the First World War. This particular example was made by C. Freidrich Ern of Solingen.

Right: Second World War vintage US Navy Utility Knife MkI with a standard issue leather sheath.

Below: This First World War push dagger by Robbins of Dudley was not official Army issue, but was supplied by private purchase to British troops. It had a slim stabbing blade nearly 5" in length, an alloy grip and a steel knucklebow.

Below: The US Navy and Marine Corps Fighting and Utility Knife MkII with its distinctive clip point blade was to become famous as the KA-BAR, no matter what company had actually made it.

Right: The US Army M3 Trench Knife, a classic design with its double edge saber point blade and stacked leather washer grip – pictured here with an M8 olive drab plastic scabbard.

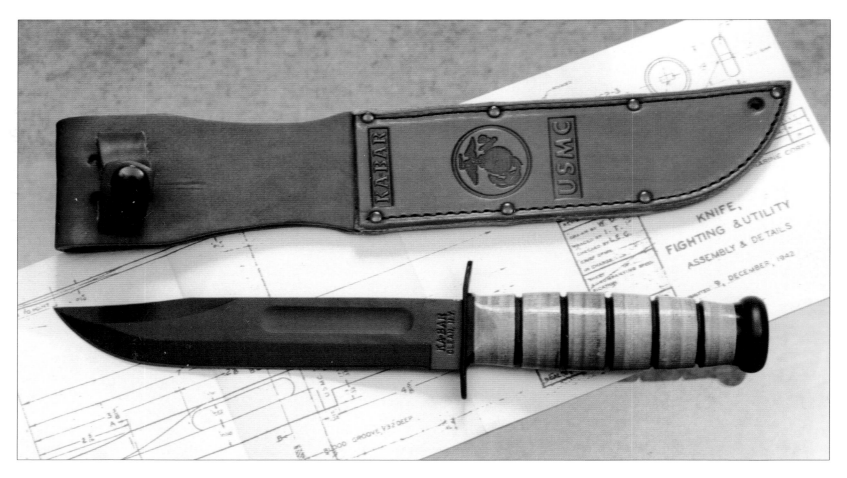

Above: A modern version of the original USMC 1219C Fighting/Utility Knife, affectionately and almost universally known as the KA-BAR. This recent model comes with a leather sheath stamped KA-BAR and USMC.

these included the Ek Commando Combat (with the great company slogan "Made in America, by Americans, for Americans"), Randall Model 1, the Marine Raider Gung Ho knife (designed for Carlson's 2d Raider Battalion), the M3 Trench Knife or Combat Knife, and, probably the most famous of them all, the USMC 1219C2 and USN MkII Fighting/Utility Knife. This knife is almost universally known as the KA-BAR.

Above: This is one of the latest KA-BAR Next Generation knives – the same overall design as the original but with stainless steel blade and manmade handle. This particular model has a part serrated blade

The KA-BAR was designed by Colonel John M. Davis and Major Howard E. America. The knife had a 7in carbon steel clip point blade with a distinctive fuller, a cross guard and compressed leather washer grip held onto the tang by a steel pommel. It was approved for service with both the US Marine Corps and the US Navy, the first batch being delivered by Camillus in January 1943. Union Cutlery also produced the knife, marking it with their KA-BAR trademark, and this name struck a chord with the Marines who used it so the name stuck, even though other companies were also engaged to supply the knife. Special plated KA-BAR knives were also issued to frogmen in US Navy UDT (Underwater Demolition Teams).

It is estimated that around one million KA-BAR knives were manufactured throughout the war, and although Union Cutlery ceased production of the KA-BAR knife following the end of hostilities, similar knives from other companies and generically named "KA-BAR" by their owners saw action in Korea, Vietnam and probably every other war since. The KA-BAR brand is now part of Alcas Corp. and has been re-established, with the original Second World War specification KA-BAR being part of the product range along with special editions and more modern adaptations of the design. The latest KA-BAR, designated the Next Generation Fighting Knife,

Above: The Fairbairn-Sykes commando dagger was designed by expert hand to hand fighters. This Second World War Pattern 2 model was made by Wilkinson Sword. It has a 6.5" double edged flattened diamond section blade.

has a stainless steel blade, a single quillon guard made of sintered low carbon stainless steel, as is the pommel, and a Kraton grip. With the senior development consultant being Greg Walker, ex-Army Ranger and Green Beret, and the editor of *Fighting Knives* magazine, no doubt this knife will continue a great tradition.

Another famous knife from the Second World War period was the Fairbairn-Sykes (F-S) British commando dagger, but there was nothing utilitarian about this design: it was made purely as a weapon. It was designed by Royal Marine Captains William E. Fairbairn and Eric A Sykes who had served with the Shanghai Municipal Police and were experienced in close fighting skills, both armed and unarmed. When put in charge of training British commandos in hand-to-hand combat, they needed a good fighting knife and turned to the designs that Fairbairn had been developing in Shanghai. The result was the British commando dagger, and although there are several variations, they all follow a generally similar pattern: a distinctive 6.75in stiletto blade, cross-guard and

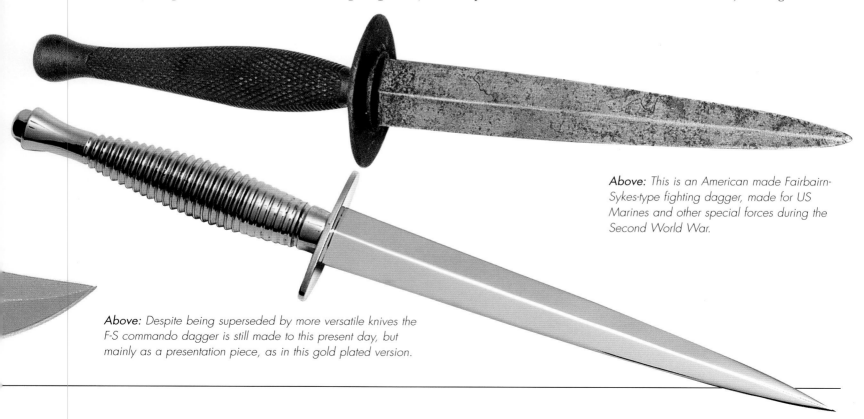

Above: This is an American made Fairbairn-Sykes-type fighting dagger, made for US Marines and other special forces during the Second World War.

Above: Despite being superseded by more versatile knives the F-S commando dagger is still made to this present day, but mainly as a presentation piece, as in this gold plated version.

Above: This is a Bill Harsey special version of the Applegate Fairbairn knife – a more useful evolutionary development of the Fairbairn-Sykes dagger. This custom model is made of 154CM steel with a fine sandblasted non-reflective surface showing the signatures of Col. Rex Applegate and Capt. William Fairbairn.

knurled one-piece metal handle with ball pommel, the whole knife being just under 12in in length. This was a formidable weapon in trained hands, but it had very little use apart from fighting. Originally made by Wilkinson Sword and several Sheffield-based cutlers, it is still in production in various decorative forms as a com-memorative item.

The commando dagger was a very important step forward in combat knife design, partly because of its effectiveness as a fighting tool, partly because of the hand-to-hand fighting techniques that came with it from its designers, Fairbairn and Sykes, but also because of its main weakness – its narrow stiletto blade didn't make a good utility knife.

When Fairbairn visited the USA to help formulate the program for training special forces and Office of Strategic Services (OSS) operatives, one of his pupils was Colonel Rex Applegate who later developed a much more practical combat knife, it having a broader spear point blade with usable sharpened edges (for fighting as well as general work). This design also had a strong tip and tang, a guard with outward-angled quillons, plus a broader, better shaped and much more comfortable handle than the straightforward Fairbairn-Sykes design. In an evolution of the F-S knife into a Fairbairn-Applegate design this last component has been particularly well thought out, with a ribbed a synthetic material (Lexan) giving a good grip and lead balance weights inside that can be adjusted to suit the user. The Fairbairn-Applegate has proved so popular that it is now made by several companies, including a special signed version by famous knifemaker Bill Harsey made with a sand-blasted 154CM steel blade hardened to Rockwell 60-61. Other knives worth looking at in this area of use are the Ek Warrior, Ontario Spec Plus SP6 and FF6 Freedom Fighter, Gerber Mk1, SOG Recon Bowie, Colt Liberator, the Cold Steel Peacekeeper and R1 Military Classic.

It was after the Second World War that we began to see the emphasis on combined fighting/utility knives as the main area of development. This is because the use of a knife as an all-round tool was becoming as important, if not more so, than as a weapon. Infantry assault weapons have become so efficient that ordinary soldiers should rarely get close enough for hand-to-hand fighting. As one British Army weapons instructor told me, "If you're close enough to use a knife, then you're too b——y close!" A similar sentiment was expressed by an old soldier who had served in Malaya

Below: The SOG Recon bowie is a reproduction of the first knife procured for special forces personnel in the Vietnam War. Like the original it is made with SK-5 gun-blued steel and has an epoxied leather handle with a brass cross-guard and pommel.

Above: The Ontario FF6 Freedom Fighter is a modern knife that has its roots in military knives such as the M3 fighting knife, but is has much more efficient hi-tech components, such as a grippy polymer handle and an 8" epoxy powder-coated carbon 1095 steel blade.

Above: *There has been a gradual increase in the use of folding knives for military/utility purposes. The Italian made Extreme Ratio Fulcrum folder is one such model, an extremely tough knife available in several blade configurations.*

during the late 1940s, and he is the only non-special forces operative that I've ever spoken to who has actually used a knife in a combat situation. On that point I have to say that, although I have spoken to hundreds of soldiers over the years, of different nationalities with experience in various wars, including a few who had experience of trench warfare in 1914–18, not one of them (apart from the one example already noted) has experienced fighting with a knife other than in training – *nor had any of them even heard of substantiated incidents of hand-to-hand knife fighting.*

No doubt there are many incidents of knife use in combat, some of them well recorded, but I am sure that almost all of them would have involved members of the various special forces units while taking part in covert operations – hence the need for a stealthy approach to eliminating an enemy. Yet, even in these circumstances, I have never heard of a "knife fight" as such. By this I mean two opposing combatants, both armed with knives. This would seem to suggest that, although such incidents may well occur and have to be prepared for, they are extremely rare, and therefore justify the move towards combination knives that are as suitable for general work as they are for fighting.

One thing that you can guarantee is that once you give anything to your average soldier he will find a way of breaking it – this goes for anything from a knife to a main battle tank. You can also guarantee that his combat knife WILL be used as a general-purpose tool

Right: *Although knife fighting situations have to be prepared for in military combat – as seen in this special forces training course from Extreme Ratio – the fact is that it very rarely occurs in modern warfare.*

for cutting, chopping, digging, hammering, etc. He will even use it as a pry-bar and, as an NCO explained to me, "Yes, soldiers do know the golden rule about not using a knife tip as a pry-bar, but they won't actually take any notice of it, even if they break the knife – because it will probably be one that they've borrowed from a mate."

So, bearing this in mind, modern combat knives are built to be strong – very strong. They must be inherently tough and they must have an edge that will stay reasonably sharp for a long time. No soldier can make his knife stronger – it either is or it isn't – but he can always put a sharper edge on it if he has to.

The strongest knives are always those made from a one piece construction, and that is the approach taken by many manufacturers for the very latest combat knives, as typified by those with full tang designs and grip scales. These include the Camillus CUDA CQB1 (Close Quarters Battle 1) and a Chris Reeve knife with the civilian name "Green Beret," but known by Green Beret special forces as "The Yarborough."

The CUDA CQB1 is a full-tang Robert Terzuola design. It is made from 5/32 thick ATS-34 steel tempered to RC59 with a matte finish. The knife has a near-6in modified saber point blade with an

Below: *The military combat/utility knife has evolved. Different manufacturers have their own ideas on final design, but a common pattern is becoming recognisable – a top quality coated steel blade and a synthetic handle, as seen here; (top) the Cold Steel Recon Scout and (bottom) the Falkniven A1.*

Above: The Camillus CUDA CQB1 is one of the new style of combat/
utility knives, using a full tang construction and Micarta grips with an
integral guard.

integral cross-guard and Black Canvas Micarta grips. CUDA, by the
way, stands for Camillus Ultra Design Advantage.

The CRK Green Beret is another good example of the type, featuring a Bill Harsey design made from one piece of CPM S30V stainless steel with the blade hardened to 55-57 Rockwell. As with the
CQB, the handle scales are in tactile Black Canvas Micarta (which

actually looks gray) and there are finger recesses shaped into the
steel for a better grip. Once again the 7in blade is best described as
a saber point, with a 6.2in edge – the first 1.25in of which is serrated – and a swaged (unsharpened) section on the drop from the spine
to the point.

Other models worthy of consideration in this more modern class
of combat/utility knives are the Al-Mar Grunt 1, Blackjack AWAC,
Buck Nighthawk, Gerber Patriot, Cold Steel Recon Scout,
Timberlite Specwar, Eickhorn ACK, SOG Tech and SOG SEAL
2000. If you're really serious about your combat knives you could

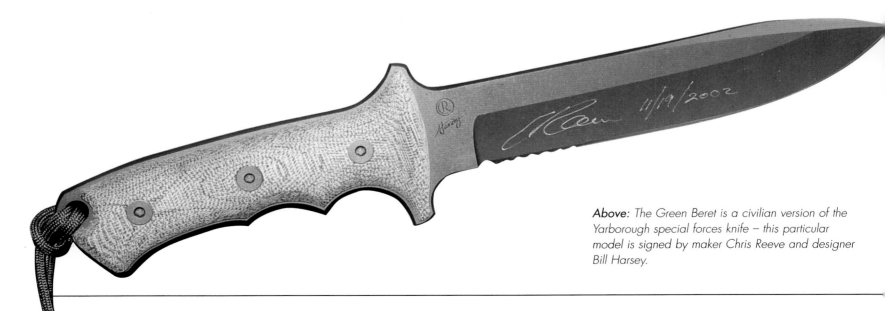

Above: The Green Beret is a civilian version of the
Yarborough special forces knife – this particular
model is signed by maker Chris Reeve and designer
Bill Harsey.

Right: This is the Kalashnikov folding knife by German knife maker Boker – it is said to be designed by Mikhail Kalashnikov of AK-47 assault rifle fame.

try the Mission Knives MPK (Multi Purpose Knife) with its non-magnetic titanium alloy blade as used by Navy SEALs for explosive ordnance disposal (EOD) work since it will not affect magnetic triggers on mines and is also virtually impervious to seawater.

One of the other important features of this type of modern knife is the relatively light weight – for instance CRK's Green Beret is just 12oz – compared to some of the larger, heavier military knives from the last quarter of the 20th century. The purpose of these was to keep the owner alive in every situation – hence their name "survival knives."

Above: The Benchmade Nimravus is another military type knife in the modern style, with a one-piece, Teflon coated full-tang 154CM stainless steel saber point blade, G10 grip scales and integral guard – note also the multi-positional Kraton sheath.

KNIVES FOR CIVILIAN SELF-DEFENSE

In contrast to the experiences of soldiers I have spoken to, unfortunately I can give several first-hand accounts of offensive knife use by civilians. These have not been knife fights; they were knife attacks, usually when an unarmed citizen was wounded by a criminal, but also in domestic disputes when a knife has been used in a moment of anger.

Note that I said "offensive" rather than "defensive." The laws of many countries forbid the carrying of a knife for defensive purposes. This may seem crazy when criminals regularly carry knives and some are prepared to use them offensively. However, there is a kind of method in the madness, since most honest citizens would contemplate carrying a knife only as a deterrent if confronted by criminals, and would not actually use it if the situation deteriorated. On the other hand, many criminals would not think twice about using a knife – and they may take yours from you.

Although the carrying of a knife for defense may be legal in some countries, I would strongly urge you not to rely on a knife as a primary means of defense. At the very least you have to be proficient in one or more of the unarmed martial arts before even contemplating the use of a knife as a defensive weapon, and even then you should undertake professional weapons training, preferably by a tutor recommended or licensed by a law enforcement agency. To quote a martial arts master and Chinese weapons expert, "Even a fool with a knife can be dangerous – to everybody around him, but mainly to himself".

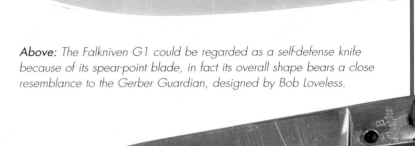

Above: *The Falkniven G1 could be regarded as a self-defense knife because of its spear-point blade, in fact its overall shape bears a close resemblance to the Gerber Guardian, designed by Bob Loveless.*

Above: *This stiletto bladed flick-knife or switchblade has a spring loaded opening mechanism, so is classified as an auto-opening knife and therefore banned or restricted in several countries.*

Some states and countries have laws restricting the advertising and sale of certain knives, including flick-knives, switchblades, gravity knives, butterfly knives (bali-songs), push daggers, belt buckle knives, knuckle-duster knives and any edged weapon that is deliberately designed to look like something else – such as a pen or a comb. To a degree this is understandable, because the link between all these knives is "concealed weapon." In the UK there are restrictions on the advertising of "combat" knives and "fighting" knives, which could affect an American knife that is one of the most popular in the world, selling by the thousand to campers, foresters and people who enjoy legitimate outdoor pursuits and sports, because the words "Fighting Knife" feature on the packaging. Somewhat ridiculously, blanking out the offending words legitimizes the sale of such knives, apparently, while some knives can be offered for sale with a simple name change (for example, the Defender II becomes the DII) because the original name might suggest a "combat" knife in the eyes of the law.

Since the awful events of September 11, 2001, it has been illegal to carry any knife (or indeed any sharp instrument) on your person or in your hand luggage onto an airplane. Yet when waiting for a flight to the UK from Nuremberg, Germany, recently, what did I notice in the airport gift shop? You guessed it, a whole range of pocket knives....

Above: *The M16 series of knives from CRKT have been specially designed for military and emergency services – the illustrated group are the versions intended for police.*

SURVIVAL KNIVES

The military approach to combat/survival knives is exemplified by the CRK Project II knife, designed in conjunction with Sergeant Karl Lippard of the US Marine Corps. The idea was to encapsulate all the features that he felt were vital for a Marine's knife. Made from a solid billet of extremely durable A2 steel, this one-piece knife has a 7.5in clip point blade hardened to 55-57RC and features a 1.5in serrated section near the ricasso, for easy cutting of cord or harness. The handle is knurled along its entire grip length, and has a cross guard at one end and an aluminum cap at the other. The cap is threaded and has an "O" ring to seal the hollow handle (4in x 0.75in approximate internal measurements). The hollow handle is also typical of what we term "survival knives," made to carry small items of kit.

One of the most famous British knives for this purpose is that known as the Wilkinson Sword survival knife, a new model of which

Left: The Dartmoor is a British made survival knife from Wilkinson Sword developed with the help of Royal Marine survival instructors.

is called the "Dartmoor." This knife has been developed with the help of Royal Marine survival instructors at the Commando Training Centre, and was introduced in March 2003 at the IWA Exhibition in Nuremberg, Germany. It has a 7.25in drop point blade, made from 440C stainless steel, with a saw profile ground along the spine. The knife is designed for heavy chopping in addition to finer cutting work, and the grip is made from high-impact nylon covered with non-slip thermoplastic rubber. The grip can be removed from the blade to reveal a survival kit tube containing a compass, metal match and a number of other survival essentials, such as fishing line, hooks, needles and the like.

Some survival knives are much simpler, like the USAF Pilot Survival Knife, which is basically a shorter version of a KA-BAR, with a saw edge on the spine and a heavier pommel for use as a hammer. It also has a utility pouch on the scabbard for carrying a sharpening stone or other small items – apparently some pilots use it to carry a small multi-tool or Swiss Army style knife instead, along with a slimline diamond hone.

Simpler still is the British MoD 4 Rescue Survival Knife, a hefty piece of kit weighing nearly 1.5lb, with a 7in long phosphate-coated carbon steel blade. This heavy-duty knife is made in Sheffield, and the latest model has a handle made from a reinforced polymer material with recessed rivets, although earlier versions had a full tang and wooden scales – not a great deal different in looks to the old trade knives that were sent to America in the 18th century!

Unfortunately, after the "Rambo" series of films, which featured

Right: A modern version of the British Army MoD (Ministry of Defence) Rescue Survival Knife has a 7" phosphated full tang carbon steel blade with stamped NATO identification number, and synthetic grip scales – some earlier models had wooden scales.

Right: The virtually indestructible Buck Master is one of the most recognisable survival knives – seen here with removable anchor pins (usually stored in the handle) screwed into the quillons.

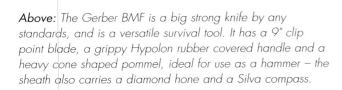

Above: *The Gerber BMF is a big strong knife by any standards, and is a versatile survival tool. It has a 9" clip point blade, a grippy Hypolon rubber covered handle and a heavy cone shaped pommel, ideal for use as a hammer – the sheath also carries a diamond hone and a Silva compass.*

a hero with an enormous bowie-style survival knife, complete with hollow handle holding enough contents to build a small house, a number of similar style knives appeared on the market. While some of the better quality models – like the Buck Master and the Gerber BMF – could be taken quite seriously, others, especially the cheaper ones, were nothing short of a joke. It could have turned out to be quite a poor joke if anybody had really depended on one of the poorer made models for their survival. But, as with many of these movie-inspired pieces of kit, they were mainly bought by dreamers and hence nobody was ever at risk.

Below: *Many survival knives, like the Buck Master, have a hollow handle for storing essential survival aids – compass, fishing kit, needles, thread, matches etc.*

At its best, a good survival knife should be able to help the owner clear vegetation, build a temporary shelter, catch and prepare food, dig a hole, start a fire, help make weapons and be a weapon in itself, plus be capable of use in a host of other duties. It is certainly asking a lot of a piece of shaped metal with an edge, and not all "survival" knives can live up to the realities of life in the outback. Luckily, real survival knives are usually required only by people who either intend to put themselves in difficult and dangerous situations – not necessarily against a human enemy – or whose work or lifestyle can suddenly land them in deep trouble. As such, there are very few people who actually need them, and those that do are usually quite aware of what's right and what's not for their particular requirements. The rest of us can survive most day-to-day problems with a simple strong knife and a good multi-tool!

RESCUE KNIVES

These are a relatively new breed of knives, designed for hard use by emergency service workers in desperate and/or dangerous situations, which means that they should handle normal everyday cutting tasks with ease. They are also tough and robust, so they are ideal for anybody who needs a heavy-duty cutting tool. They might even help to save a life if a real emergency is encountered.

I used to work as a steel erector/rigger on power stations and oil refineries, and as I was also an occupational first-aider I was often drafted into the site rescue squad. Part of the equipment that I considered to be absolutely essential was a good knife (which is essential for a rigger anyway). Most of the time I carried a British Army style jack-knife and, although I cannot claim to have directly saved any lives with it, it certainly helped to save at least two limbs (a hand and a leg in separate incidents). Any sharp, reliable knife would have done at a pinch, but

Above: The Cold Steel Land & Sea Rescue is a simple knife with a tough serrated sheep's foot blade, ideal for safe (if sometimes untidy) cutting of virtually any material – if it can be cut with a knife, then this knife will cut it.

Above: The features of the Eickhorn PRT-II make it a potential life saver – a good choice for emergency service workers or just for keeping in your car.

nowadays there are specifically designed knives available for emergency service workers.

The Land & Sea Rescue knife by Cold Steel is an example of one of the simpler models, having a stainless steel serrated locking blade, a tough, non-slip handle made of Zytel with a molded integral pocket clip and a lanyard hole. The knife can be opened with one hand using the ambidextrous stud through the spine of the blade. The break-back lock holds the blade securely and it can be closed easily by applying pressure to the thumb cut-out on the back of the handle. The blade has a sheep's-foot tip to offer a degree of puncture protection when cutting close to people in emergency situations (cutting automobile seat-belts, for example), or if the open knife is accidentally dropped. The blade has two types of serrations – fine and coarse – for all of its length apart from approximately a half-inch of plain edge just before the sheep's-foot tip. The AUS 8A stainless steel blade zips through most sheet materials – including light gauge metal at a push…but obviously this should only be done in a real emergency, and expect a whole lot of restoration work after this type of abuse. In addition, this type of blade will handle most rope, cord and light metal wire materials, as well as small branches and other natural fibers.

I have been using one of these knives for about three to four years

Right: Apart from an excellent blade, the PRT-II has a slotted seat belt cutter and a hardened stud on the handle base for glass breaking.

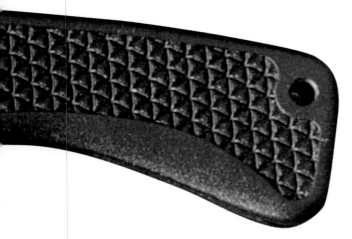

now, and the blade has stayed incredibly sharp with very little maintenance (i.e., virtually none), while the all stainless steel and Zytel construction ensures that the knife stays corrosion-free. The finer serrations can "clog" when cutting some fine fibers, causing a temporary reduction in sharpness, but the larger serrations will still carry on cutting, and the blade's usual keen edge is easily regained with simple cleaning.

The Original PRT-II by Eickhorn is a very classy piece of kit from Solingen in Germany, and is just one of a whole range of rescue knives that they make for fire-fighters, police and paramedics. PRT stands for "pocket rescue tool" and it is a folding knife design (with a liner lock) especially developed for those who prefer a lightweight compact knife. The company also make heavy-duty fixed blade rescue knives. The PRT has a utility blade, half serrated and half plain in 440A stainless steel. It also has a safe recessed seat-belt cutter in the handle that can even be used with the knife in the closed position. However, if the victim were to be trapped by rope or similar

materials (as occurred in a very serious accident that I attended) the seat belt cutter would be useless, since it is designed to cut only flat materials. So you would need to use the knife's main blade, and in this situation the best design is one that doesn't have such a pronounced point.

Another version of a rescue knife is the First Response by Smith & Wesson. This model is designed by well known bladesmith, Blackie Collins. He is a fairly uncompromising character when it comes to his work, so you can bet that this knife has been well thought out. The First Response is really a specialist tool and the latest version has a totally new blade design compared to older models I've seen. The blade has a blunted tip for safety, but the unusual concave blade has a scalloped edge ground from both sides. The new design keeps the rounded tip – which can also be used as a screwdriver or a pry bar in an emergency. It is the only example I know of a manufacturer encouraging this kind of use – but anything goes in an emergency, and the stainless steel axis pin for the blade is a quarter-inch in diameter to offer maximum resistance to blade/handle separation. The 440 stainless steel blade may look strange but it is incredibly sharp, despite its unusual shape. A checkered steel stud on each side of the blade helps easy opening with either hand, and it is held open with a liner lock. Another unusual feature is a spring-loaded steel bolt with a hardened tip for breaking toughened glass, such as that found on auto windscreens or double glazing.

New models of rescue knife are being introduced all the time. There's no doubt that this area of knife ownership is getting bigger. This type of knife is now being carried by many automobile owners and truck drivers in the glove compartments of their vehicles, as well as by emergency service professionals.

Below: The S&W First Response really is a specialist rescue tool, with features such as the captive bolt glass breaker and the unusual safety blade that can double as a pry-bar in an emergency.

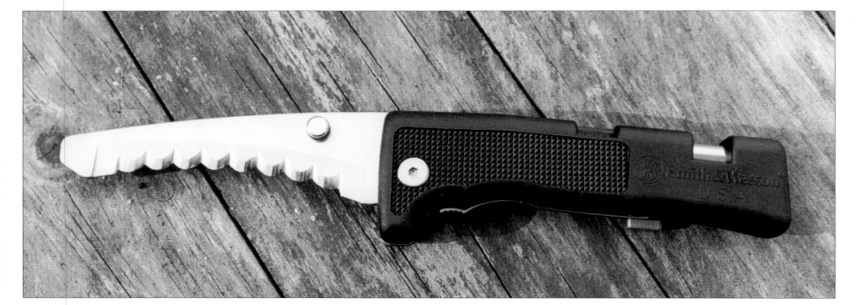

Collecting Knives

As I explained earlier, I'm not a knife collector – nevertheless, I can certainly see the attraction of the hobby. A collector's interest in a knife can be based on its quality or rarity, or sometimes because it is representative of a type from a particular historic or ethnic background. In addition, there is also a great deal of interest in collecting knives from specific manufacturers or individual makers.

HISTORIC KNIVES

Although there is a market for ancient flint, copper and bronze knives, it is a very specialized field of interest. Such knives are mainly offered in sales of established collections – however, individual items may crop up from time to time at general sales, and some prices can be surprisingly modest. In contrast, early Iron Age knives – when offered in good condition – can often be extraordinarily expensive, simply because most surviving examples tend to be badly corroded. This also applies to many iron and steel knives from the 1st to the 10th centuries AD. Later steel knives, from medieval times onwards, are much more likely to be encountered and can be found in fair to excellent condition.

From about 1200 AD onwards, specialist cutlers started to settle in Sheffield in England, Solingen in Germany and Thiers in France, all of which are now considered centers of excellence for knifemaking. Many different types of knives were made, and it should be remembered that for the nobility a dagger was part of court dress, and was therefore also considered to be a fashion item, leading to some very elaborately decorated designs. Examples of the more commonly recognised medieval styles of knife, such as ballock daggers and rondels, sometimes appear at large sales of antique arms and armor, with prices reflecting both the condition and rarity. Baselards and ear daggers are less frequently seen for sale, so will

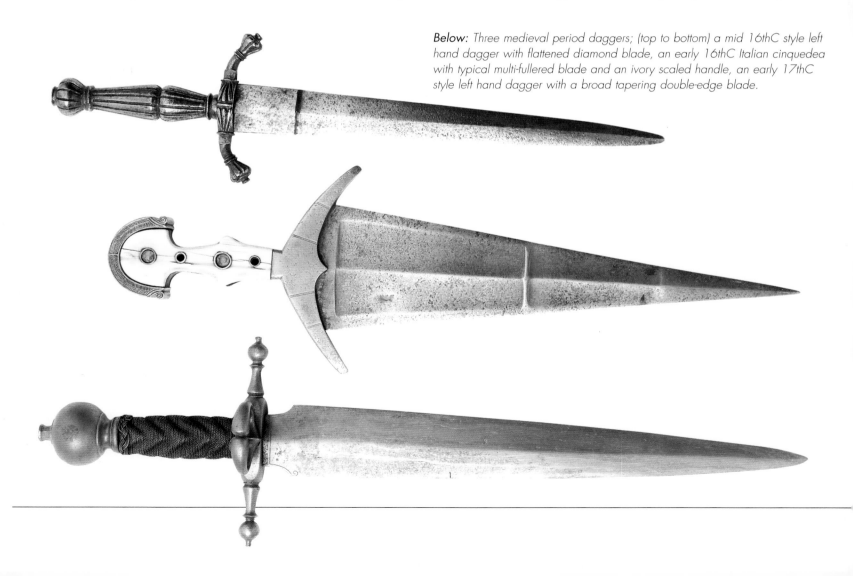

Below: Three medieval period daggers; (top to bottom) a mid 16thC style left hand dagger with flattened diamond blade, an early 16thC Italian cinquedea with typical multi-fullered blade and an ivory scaled handle, an early 17thC style left hand dagger with a broad tapering double-edge blade.

fetch correspondingly higher prices.

For five hundred years general designs did not change much, with daggers featuring quillons (cross guard arms) and a double-edged blade being a common trait, especially in the various main gauche or sword parrying types. The 15th to 16th century Italian cinquedea is a notable exception, being very distinctive, with its wide fluted blade (the name cinquedea refers to the blade being five fingers wide) and gladius style hilt.

EATING IRONS

Iron and steel cutlery was relatively expensive in ancient times and, since they were not provided in inns, Roman and Greek travelers would carry their own knives for eating, and sometimes spoons and/or two-pronged forks. Although innkeepers started to supply eating implements when mass production made them cheaper, the practice of carrying your own eating knife continued well into the 20th century, especially among itinerant workers in Mediterranean countries.

Left: Some typical collectible medieval daggers; (left to right) 15th/16thC ballock or kidney dagger (so-called because of the characteristic protuberances forming the guard on the handle), a 17th/18thC dagger with hollow triangular section blade and Spanish or Scandinavian carved boxwood handle, a 15thC rondel dagger with ivory hilt, a 15thC dagger with slender flattened diamond section blade and Y-shaped ivory handle, a 15thC style dagger with flattened hexagonal section blade, small steel guard, wooden spiral grip and brass pommel.

Below: A highly decorated late 17thC Spanish version of a left hand dagger, complete with covered guard and ricasso with "sword breaking" notches on either side.

Right: An antique Scottish dirk set, complete with corresponding miniature knife and fork, and scabbard.

THE DIRK AND THE SKEAN DHU

Probably the most recognizable knife shape from the 17th to 18th centuries is the dirk (derived from the earlier ballock daggers) as typified by the traditional fighting knife worn by officers of Scottish Highland regiments for over 200 years. The dirk has a dagger-like blade and the grips are generally made of ebony, usually carved in a basket-work pattern (or Celtic knots on very early versions), with the pommel surmounted by a cairngorm (a semi-precious stone, often amber or amethyst). The leather scabbard is reinforced with wood and has two small openings on the front to carry a small knife and fork which matched the dirk. These sets are often richly decorated with engraved brass or silver mounts and pins.

It is customary for the dirk to be accompanied by a matching skean dhu or sgian dubh (pronounced skeen doo), a small knife worn in the top of a stocking as part of the highlander's traditional dress. The name means black knife (from Gaelic skean – dagger, and dhu – black). Although the knife usually has a black handle, it is generally reckoned that black in this context is meant as dark, hidden or secret. This could refer to a hidden dagger carried under a jacket in the armpit by Scots in the 18th century, supposedly because the English would not let them carry arms.

Military dirks and skean dhus will usually have a regimental

Above: A richly decorated Highland dirk set, with a matching skean dhu – note the "cairngorms," semi-precious stones forming the pommels of the knives.

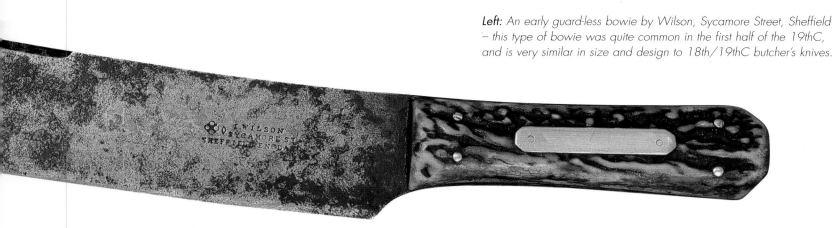

Left: An early guard-less bowie by Wilson, Sycamore Street, Sheffield – this type of bowie was quite common in the first half of the 19thC, and is very similar in size and design to 18th/19thC butcher's knives.

badge and battle honors somewhere on the knives and/or scabbards. Antique military and civilian dirk sets are both highly prized, and good examples will often fetch exceptional prices at auction.

THE BOWIE KNIFE

Very few edged weapons have become so famous that their names have become common parlance, and there is only one that has carried the name of its original owner from the early 19th century right through to the present day. That is the bowie knife, as first carried by the famous frontiersman, James Bowie.

In the early 1800s it was common for men on the frontier to carry a large knife – often known as a butcher's knife – as a sidearm and general tool, but it was not until around 1830, after the Sandbar Duel on the Mississippi, that James Bowie's knife became famous, spawning thousands of copies and creating a permanent place for itself and its owner in American folklore.

Born in Kentucky around 1796, James Bowie was one of ten children of a Scottish/American father and Welsh mother. By 1801 the family was living in Louisiana, with a successful plantation and ranch. James was particularly close to his brothers, Rezin and John. He is described as being tall and strong, with sandy hair, gray eyes and a fair complexion. His character was said to be complex; he was open, frank and friendly, but he could also be secretive and ruthless, and had an awesome temper when roused. He made quite a few enemies in his business dealings, with a certain Major John Norris Wright, a banker and sheriff, being one of them. In 1826 Bowie was shot by Norris Wright – but luckily the ball was deflected. Later, in 1827, using his knife, Bowie killed the major at the Sandbar Duel (see separate account) and possibly as a result of this he headed off west to Texas (then a Mexican territory). While in Texas he was said to have been attacked by three hired killers – but he killed two of them and badly wounded the third, all with his knife.

After this incident, the Sandbar Duel and Bowie's many other

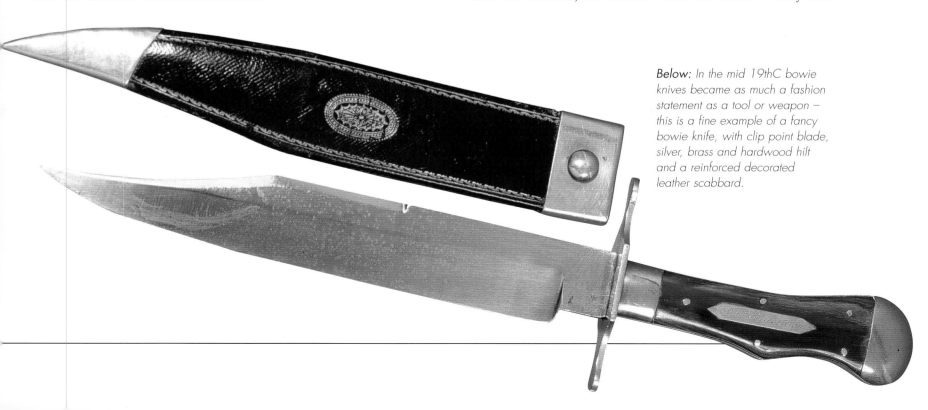

Below: In the mid 19thC bowie knives became as much a fashion statement as a tool or weapon – this is a fine example of a fancy bowie knife, with clip point blade, silver, brass and hardwood hilt and a reinforced decorated leather scabbard.

Below: An I*XL bowie style knife with typical blade and cross-guard, circa 1955, manufactured by George Wostenholm & Son, Washington Works, Sheffield – where bowie knives have been made since the second quarter of the 1800s, when James Bowie was still alive.

Below: When bowie knives became popular in the early to mid 19thC, the demand was massive, so many European knife manufacturers stepped in to supply the needs of the American market – this is a German example, with typical long clip point blade, a stag antler handle and a reinforced leather scabbard with metal throat and belt clip.

reported exploits while fighting Indians, his name and his knife became equally famous. Public demand for Bowie-style knives was met with great enthusiasm by American blacksmiths and cutlers in the various settled territories and states across the continent. Some of these makers achieved exquisite levels of decorative quality, while others merely churned out plain, sturdy butcher knives. In addition, many thousands of knives were supplied to the American market from Europe. The Sheffield cutlery industry in particular was quick to exploit this fashion for large knives, although some of the attempts at authenticity were more fanciful than practical. It is said that James Bowie himself placed an order for twelve knives from George Wostenholm & Son Ltd., and there is a commemorative knife from this Sheffield manufacturer on show at the Alamo museum, San Antonio, Texas, although in fact it was made long after Bowie's death.

As a colonel of "Texican" militia James Bowie joined the cause of Texas independence. Along with Col. William Travis, Col. Davy Crockett and a group of fewer than 200 volunteers, Bowie went to defend the Alamo mission in San Antonio against General Santa Anna and a Mexican army of some 5,000 troops. James Bowie was killed on or around March 6, 1836 – although he was already very ill, possibly with pneumonia or tuberculosis, and probably never

Above: *Another fancy bowie with a long clip point blade, mother of pearl scales, silver mounts and pins – this type of knife was a fashionable accessory in the Southern states and on the Mississippi riverboats of the 19thC.*

actually took part in the fighting.

The Daughters of the Republic of Texas, who maintain the Alamo as a shrine and museum, say that Bowie's knife was never recovered. Although several bowie-type knives are on display at the Alamo, none of them is claimed to be the original knife carried by James Bowie.

The exact design of the knife has been disputed. Nevertheless, the term "bowie knife" has now become a generic name for any large hunting and/or fighting knife with a clip point blade. Most historic accounts agree that the bowie knife was indeed large and heavy, with a brass cross-guard and a single, razor-sharp edge consisting of a substantial belly curving up to a clip point. The thick spine was unbeveled except for the clip, which had either a false concave edge or was beveled but unsharpened.

Some other accounts claim that the original bowie knife was a double-edged, dagger-type weapon, the sort that is now known as an Arkansas Toothpick. This idea has generally been discredited, but there are still plenty of 19th century European- and even American-made knives that fit this description, yet they are still described in catalogs as "bowie knives." In fact these knives could be of any design, single- or double-edge, spear or clip point, with or without a cross-guard and having straight, curved, serpentine or coffin-shaped handles.

Just as there are many theories as to what the original knife looked like, there are as many claims as to who designed and/or made it. One would have thought that the most authoritative would come from James's own brothers. However, while Rezin Bowie

DRACULA – THE AMERICAN AND NEPALESE CONNECTIONS

In Bram Stoker's novel "Dracula" the infamous vampire wasn't killed with a wooden stake – it was an American bowie knife that was driven through the evil Count's heart, while at the same time his neck was completely severed with a Nepalese kukri!

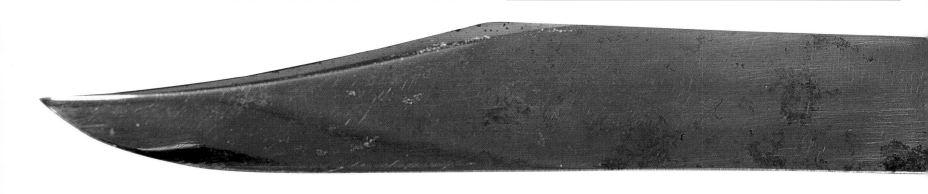

Below: The bowie knife is generally regarded as having a clip point blade, while the "Arkansas Toothpick" (as seen here) is said to have a long spear point, saber point or tapering blade, but in collection and auction catalogs you may find a lot of cross over between the two types.

claimed to have designed a straight-edged knife and had it made by the local blacksmith, Jesse Clift, his brother John claimed that a blacksmith named Snowdon made the knife.

It appears to me that the bowie knife as we know it today is a collective result of a progression of knife designs. The forerunners of the generally accepted bowie design can be seen in the European and American trade and butcher knives, common all over the Western frontier of the early 19th century. A curved clip point and deep belly can also be seen in Spanish-derived knife designs from Mexico.

It is accepted that James Bowie may have had copies of his knife made for friends and dignitaries, so it is possible that more than one blacksmith or cutler made knives of the type for him. One thing is for sure; after Jim Bowie's famous demise at the Alamo, any blacksmith who so much as shoed Bowie's horse would surely have been tempted to claim he also made that famous knife.

RIOTOUS ASSEMBLY?

In 1837 at the first session of the Arkansas General Assembly, the Speaker, John Wilson, killed Major J. J. Anthony, another legislator, on the floor of the house after a dispute about a new law (concerned with wolf hunting). Both men were armed with bowie knives and Wilson was also badly wounded during the fight. Wilson was arrested for murder and expelled from the House of Representatives, but was acquitted at trial and eventually re-elected.

BANNING THE BOWIE

Following the rapidly growing popularity - and growing public fear - of the bowie knife in the mid to late 1830s, State laws were brought about specifically banning the bowie knife in Alabama (1837) and Tennessee (1838). Less specific dueling laws, that nevertheless named the bowie knife, were also enacted in Mississippi (1837).

Below: This knife is described as a bowie, but it has an 11" saber point blade – it was made in Sheffield by Wade, Wingfield & Rowbotham. In the 19thC it was common practice to describe any large knife as a bowie to increase its saleability on the American market.

Left: A German made bowie style hunting knife with unusual fullered 10" clip blade, marked with a crown and star logo, the handle featuring a boar's head carved pommel.

Below: A fine example of a "coffin handle bowie" – a popular style made famous by San Francisco cutlers during the California gold rush. This particular knife with horn handle inlay and lion decorated pommel was made by S. Wragg & Sons, Furnace Hill, Sheffield.

THE SANDBAR DUEL

How this duel came about is not really relevant here; suffice to say that a certain Samuel Levi Wells had a dispute with a Dr. Thomas H. Maddox, and they decided to settle their differences in a duel on September 19, 1827, on a sandbar (possibly Vidalia Island) in the Mississippi River, at a crossing point between Natchez, Mississippi, and Vidalia, Louisiana.

Apart from their official "seconds" each man had brought a group of friends. Maddox was accompanied by Major John Norris Wright, Colonel Robert Crain, Alfred Blanchard, Edward Blanchard and Dr. Denny, among others. Samuel Wells's party included James Bowie, Thomas Wells, General Samuel Cuney, Dr. Cuney and George Whorter.

Under the formalized (yet illegal) dueling rules of the time, Wells and Maddox exchanged shots, but neither hit his target. They reloaded and fired again, both missing once more. It was agreed that honor had been served and the two opponents decided to shake hands and bring the matter to a close. Unfortunately, the two opposing factions accompanying them were not satisfied, and the duel degenerated into a brawl.

Most reports confirm the main points of the following step-by-step account, but the sequence of events and the particular details must still be open to question.

Bowie fired at Robert Crain and missed. Crain replied with two shots, putting one through Bowie's hip, while the other killed Samuel Cuney. Bowie then pulled his "large butcher's knife," but Crain felled him with a blow to the head from the butt of a pistol. Maddox then tried to pin Bowie down but was pushed off. Norris Wright then shot Bowie through the lower chest but, still on the floor, Bowie fired back, hitting Norris Wright. Alfred Blanchard and Norris Wright then attacked Bowie (with knives, swords or sword sticks, depending on which account you read), stabbing him several times. But as Norris Wright bent over "to finish him off," Bowie plunged his knife through his opponent's chest, then raised himself and slashed Alfred Blanchard severely. Edward Blanchard then shot Bowie in the thigh and was himself shot and wounded by Wells. The fight broke up, with a claimed six dead and fifteen wounded. Amazingly, Bowie, against all the odds, was still alive.

At this point – if you include the attack by Major Norris Wright the year before – Bowie had survived at least four bullets, several knife/sword wounds and a bludgeoning attack to his skull…. If only half this information is correct, it suggests that James Bowie was one tough cookie.

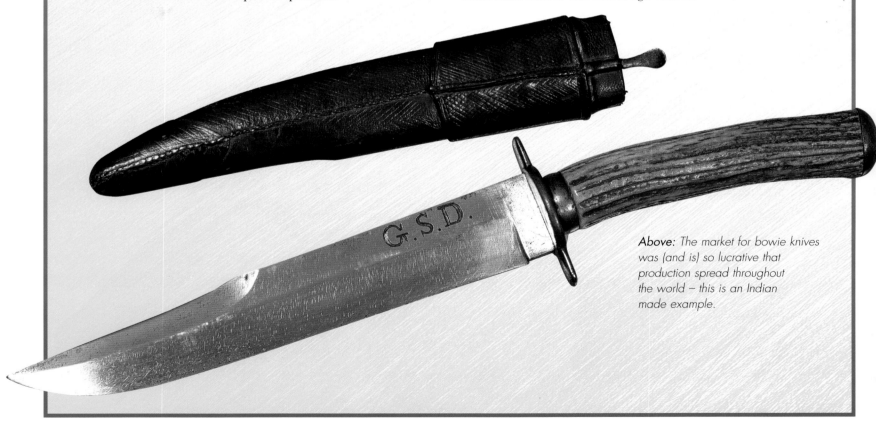

Above: *The market for bowie knives was (and is) so lucrative that production spread throughout the world – this is an Indian made example.*

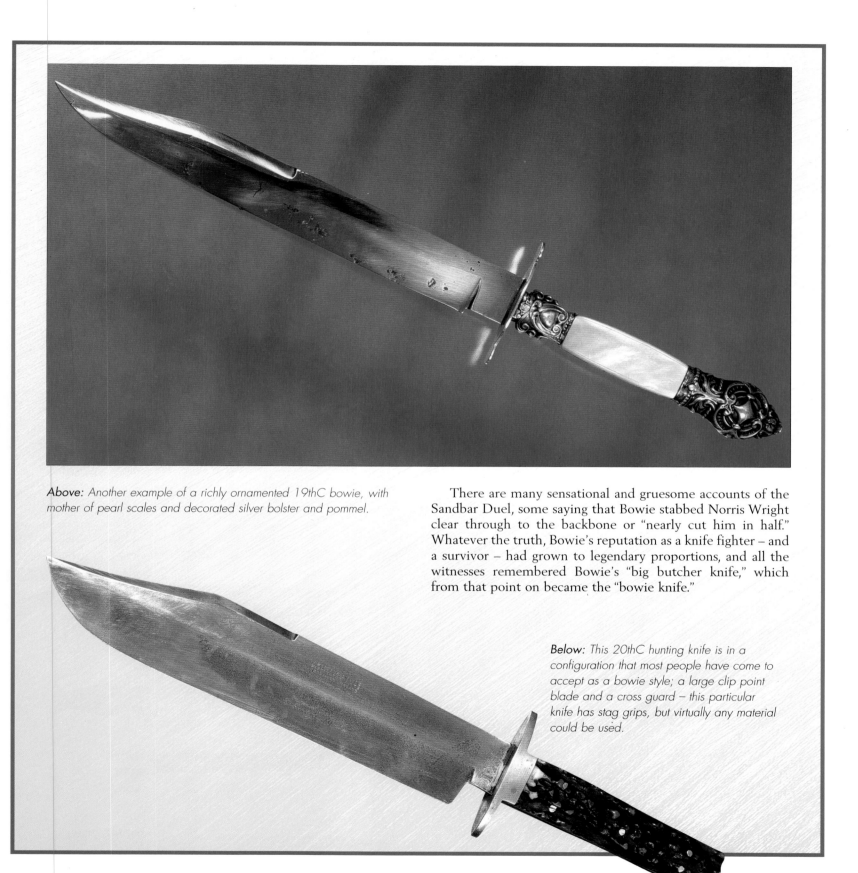

Above: Another example of a richly ornamented 19thC bowie, with mother of pearl scales and decorated silver bolster and pommel.

There are many sensational and gruesome accounts of the Sandbar Duel, some saying that Bowie stabbed Norris Wright clear through to the backbone or "nearly cut him in half." Whatever the truth, Bowie's reputation as a knife fighter – and a survivor – had grown to legendary proportions, and all the witnesses remembered Bowie's "big butcher knife," which from that point on became the "bowie knife."

Below: This 20thC hunting knife is in a configuration that most people have come to accept as a bowie style; a large clip point blade and a cross guard – this particular knife has stag grips, but virtually any material could be used.

DRESS KNIVES OF THE AXIS POWERS

Most military knives and bayonets are regarded as collectible, and none more so than those of the German Third Reich. During Hitler's Nazi regime of the 1930s and 40s there was a resurgence in ceremonial dagger (and sword) production at the famous cutlery making center of Solingen, which had suffered badly from the global economic depression of the previous decade. The governing National Socialist Party (Nazis) "awarded" ceremonial daggers to officers, NCOs and men from every section of military service, especially the SA (Sturmabteilung or Storm Troopers, commonly known as "Brownshirts") and later the SS (Schutzstaffel – the Elite Guard), and also to party members from all corners of civil society. These daggers and dirks were decorated with Nazi emblems, runic symbols and the like, becoming an important part of Nazi regalia and a link to the weapons of their legendary heroes – the Teutonic knights. SA

and SS Nazi daggers took the shape of the medieval baselard as a pattern.

The Italian fascists under Mussolini also prized ceremonial edged weapons, but were nowhere near as widespread or prolific in their distribution compared to the Nazis in Germany. Naturally enough, the design of Italian daggers sought to suggest links between the fascist political doctrine and the Roman Empire.

The militaristic society of Japan, up until the end of the Second World War, traditionally had more interest in swords than knives, though dirks were issued to virtually all service officers. Dirks were also given to high-ranking officials of civilian services, such as police, fire fighters, railway workers, and even the Red Cross. Probably the most famous Japanese military knife is the kamikaze dirk as presented to suicide pilots in the Navy Air Force. These were relatively short, plain knives without a guard – and the generic name aikuchi is used for Japanese knives of this type. The kamikaze pilots took

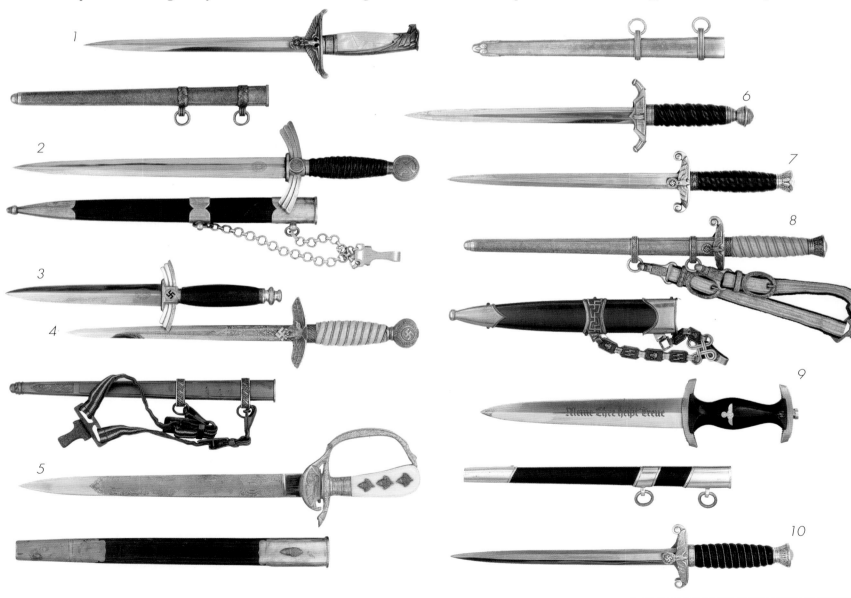

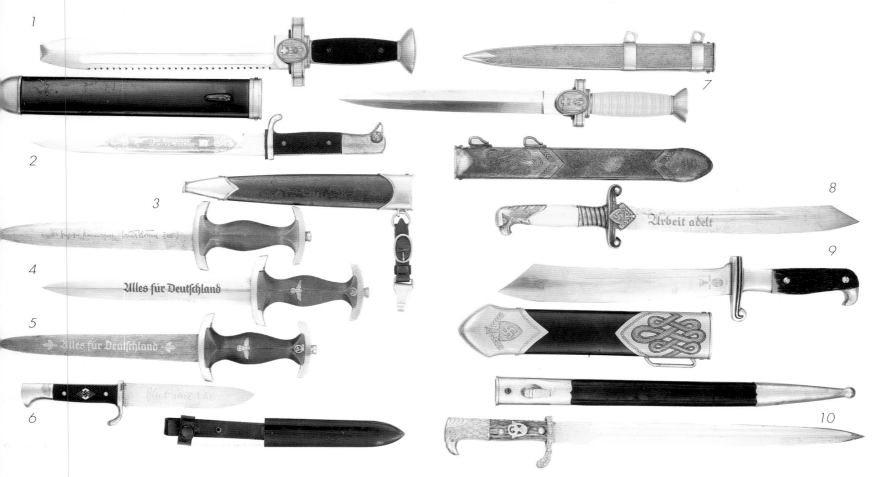

Left: 1. Third Reich Government (Foreign Office) official's dagger with 10.25" blade, mother of pearl scales, silver decoration and silver plated sheath – the Diplomatic Service dagger is almost identical, but with the Nazi eagle on the cross guard (not the eagle's head on the pommel) facing the other way.

2. Luftwaffe (Air Force) dagger, 1934 pattern, for officers and NCOs, near 12" blade with silver mounted blue leather sheath.

3. Deutsche Luftsport Verband (DLV – the German air sports association) dagger, made by Josef Münch, Brotterode.

4. Third Reich Luftwaffe (Air Force) officer's dagger 1937 pattern with etched 10.125" blade, aluminum cross guard and pommel.

5. Reichsforstamt (National Forestry Service) Senior Forester's cutlass type sidearm with etched 13" single edge blade, decorated knucklebow hilt with ivory scales (junior ranks daggers had stag horn scales).

6. Third Reich Bahnschutzpolizei (Railway Protection Police) 1938 pattern dagger with 10.25" blade – similar to the standard Army dagger but with railway insignia on cross guard and a black plastic grip.

7. Third Reich Heer (Army) dagger, but with Bahnschutzpolizei type black grip – the normal grip would be cream or orange.

8. Standard pattern Third Reich Heer (Army) dagger and sheath.

9. Shutzestaffel (SS Protection Dept.) officer's dagger 1936 pattern.

10. Third Reich (Customs Service) official's dagger with similar size blade and pommel as the standard Army issue, but a slightly different cross piece (the eagle on this model has upturned wings).

Right: 1. Third Reich Rotes Kreuz (Red Cross) first aid man's dress dagger, with broad 10.5" fullered, saw backed, chisel tipped blade.

2. Third Reich private purchase dress bayonet, the blade is single-edged and is etched "Zur Erinnerung an meine Dienstzeit" (In memory of my service time).

3. Sturmabteilungen (SA) dagger, 1933 pattern, bearing the inscription on the reverse side "In herzlicher Freundschaft Ernst Rohm" (In heartfelt friendship, Ernst Rohm), but after the "Night of the Long Knives" in June 1934 when SA chief Ernst Rohm and a number of other SA leaders were murdered by the SS, many SA men threw their daggers away or ground the inscription off – so this dagger is quite rare.

4. Obverse side of Sturmabteilungen dagger (see No.3).

5. Sturmabteilungen (SA) dagger with damascus blade and "Alles für Deutschland" in gold – the cost was about forty times that of the standard dagger, so this is a very rare knife.

6. Hitlerjugend (HJ – Hitler Youth) knife, with 5.5" blade.

7. Third Reich Rotes Kreuz (Red Cross) officer's dagger, with double edged 9.9" blade.

8. Reichsarbeitsdienst (RAD – National Labour Service) officer's dagger, the 10.25 blade bearing the inscription "Arbeit adelt" (Labour ennobles).

9. Reichsarbeitsdienst (RAD – National Labour Service) man's dagger, the 9.9" blade marked with RAD triangle emblem and maker – Carl Julius Krebs.

10. Third Reich Polizei (Police) sidearm. This was like a dress bayonet but without an attachment for mounting to a rifle.

their knives on missions during which they would try to crash their planes into enemy ships, so for obvious reasons their knives are extremely rare.

KNIVES OF THE WORLD

Although knives are the commonest tools of man, they have developed differently in various countries for many diverse reasons – local materials, particular usage or just plain fashion. Because of this they can make interesting subjects for the collector, and since many companies continue to make knives in the traditional styles of their own countries of origin, it can be gratifying to assemble a representative selection of modern knives to form the basis of a collection. Some of the following, knives, particularly those from Africa, Arabia and Asia, are usually pursued only as antiques. Folding knives from Britain, Germany and the USA are not included here, since they are covered in other chapters.

AFRICA, ARABIA AND ASIA

There are literally dozens of different types of knives and daggers from countries in these two great continents, and many of the individual types can be subdivided into particular regions; it is not within the scope of this book to discuss them all. Moreover, some "knives" from these regions, such as the Philippine barong, are so large that they should really be classed as swords. The following are some of the main collectible knives that can be readily identified;

The dha from Burma and Thailand can be anything from ten inches overall right up to sword length; the straight blade can be plain or damascened, the hilt may be ivory or silver-covered wood.

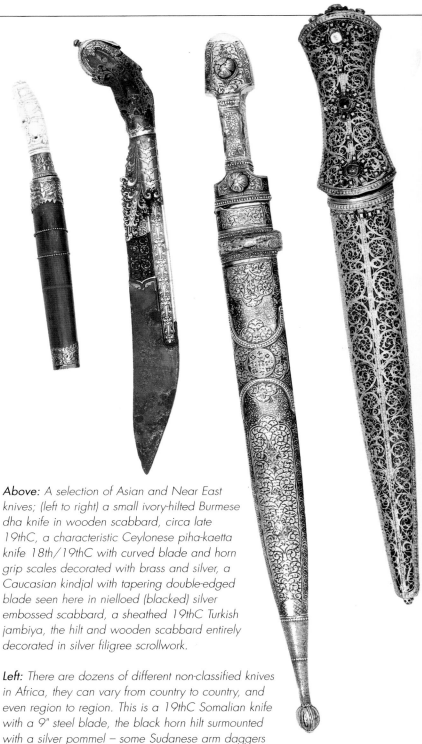

Above: A selection of Asian and Near East knives; (left to right) a small ivory-hilted Burmese dha knife in wooden scabbard, circa late 19thC, a characteristic Ceylonese piha-kaetta knife 18th/19thC with curved blade and horn grip scales decorated with brass and silver, a Caucasian kindjal with tapering double-edged blade seen here in nielloed (blacked) silver embossed scabbard, a sheathed 19thC Turkish jambiya, the hilt and wooden scabbard entirely decorated in silver filigree scrollwork.

Left: There are dozens of different non-classified knives in Africa, they can vary from country to country, and even region to region. This is a 19thC Somalian knife with a 9" steel blade, the black horn hilt surmounted with a silver pommel – some Sudanese arm daggers can be of a similar shape but much smaller.

The sheath is usually of wood with a decorated silver covering.

The katar or punch dagger from India was designed for piercing chain mail, and is unusual in that it may have one or three blades (the latter fanning out when the twin grip bars are squeezed).

The khanjar is commonly found in both Arabia and the Indian sub-continent. It is normally 12 to15 inches overall, with a recurved blade and a pistol grip handle. The knife and can be plain or ornate.

Below: This katar has a fullered steel blade and a brass handle with twin elongated barrel shaped gripping bars.

Above: Large and small versions of the Indian katar dagger – the twin cross bars (these ones are diamond section) are held in a fist like grip and the weapon is "punched" forward.

Right: Two Indian khanjali (or khanjarli) daggers, circa 18thC, with their recurved blades and distinctive fan shaped pommels – the top version has a knucklebow guard.

Below: This Indonesian Kris has the typical wide triangular blade base at the handle joint, and the very distinctive scabbard with boat shaped throat – this particular model is silver mounted. Some versions have a wavy blade.

Below: This high quality jambiya has a silver hilt, silver scabbard, and gold inlay decoration on a watered steel blade.

Below: A modern presentation jambiya with gold hilt in an L-shaped Arabian style decorated gold scabbard. (Photo courtesy of Wallis & Wallis)

Below: Two curved North African daggers – (top) a narrow version of the jambiya, possibly Moroccan, and (bottom) a richly decorated jambiya in an ornate scabbard.

The khanjarli is an Indian version with a fan-shaped pommel.

The kris, from Malaya and Indonesia, is a long-bladed dagger, sometimes with a serpentine blade, and usually a carved wooden handle. The scabbard is unusual in having a broad, deep "boat-like" throat. A longer, sword-type version was used by Moro tribesmen in the Philippines.

The jambiya is the quintessential Arabian dagger, being found throughout the whole of the Middle East, North Africa and Indian subcontinent, even spreading into the Balkans. It can be from 12 to 16 inches overall, with a distinctive curved blade and matching curved or L-shaped scabbard. The handle flares at the juncture with the blade to form a guard, but there are no quillons. The blade will often be damascene (watered) or engraved and the handle is usually ornate – sometimes decorated with silver or gold and set with semi

precious stones. The Moroccan koummya dagger is of a similar shape but generally narrower.

The kard is found from Turkey to Afghanistan and is a narrow, straight-bladed, single-edge dagger usually with a forged bolster but no cross-guard. The Moroccan khodmi is very similar, as are some Mediterranean daggers.

The pesh-kabz from northern India, Afghanistan and Persia (Iran) is similar to the kard but has a concave edge, making it even narrower and more useful for piercing chain mail.

JAPAN

There are several complete volumes on studying and collecting each of the Japanese knife types such as aikuchi, kaiken, kozuka and

THE GURKHA KNIFE

The kukri is probably the most famous knife from Nepal in Asia, being a combined fighting knife and working tool. It is the symbol of one of the most famous British Army units, the Ghurkas. Its unique shape is easily recognizable, distinguishing it from all other knives. It is the longest serving edged sidearm in the world, and it still is used as a weapon, rather than part of ceremonial regalia.

The kukri is still handmade in its native Nepal at the foot of the Himalayas. It is made in several different sizes and styles, the blades usually measuring from 11 to 14 inches long. In the hands of expert Gurkhas the curved blade concentrates

maximum weight at point of impact. The slimmer-bladed versions are called sirapati, while the fullered-blade types are known as angkola. The handle is normally of carved polished wood, but can also be made of brass. Kukri are usually found complete with two matching accessory blades – a little skinner/utility knife (the karda) and a sharpening steel (the chakma). The traditional scabbard is of wood wrapped in water buffalo hide.

Above: This ceremonial quality 19thC ivory handled kukri with silver mounted case was presented to Regimental Sergeant Major William Gower of the North Bengal Mounted Rifles.

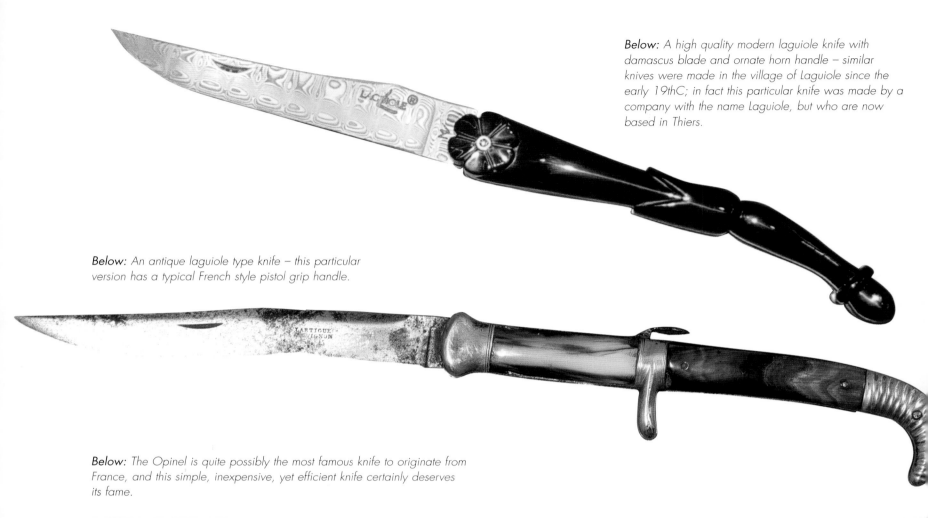

Below: A high quality modern laguiole knife with damascus blade and ornate horn handle – similar knives were made in the village of Laguiole since the early 19thC; in fact this particular knife was made by a company with the name Laguiole, but who are now based in Thiers.

Below: An antique laguiole type knife – this particular version has a typical French style pistol grip handle.

Below: The Opinel is quite possibly the most famous knife to originate from France, and this simple, inexpensive, yet efficient knife certainly deserves its fame.

Above: A damascus bladed "Gobbo Abruzze" knife made by Conaz Coltellerie – Gobbo means "hunchback" and refers to the curved handle, while Abruzze indicates that the design originally comes from Abruzzi in Southern Italy.

tanto. It is too complex a subject for discussion here, but I can recommend the book *Samurai* by Clive Sinclaire (published by Salamander Books).

FRANCE

The town of Thiers is the largest cutlery center in France, although there have been others. For instance, the laguiole knife is named after the village of its origin in southern France. This clasp knife was created by Pierre-Jean Calmels in 1829, using the black horn of the local aubrac cattle for the handle. It looks similar to the navaja knife, which Calmels probably saw being used by Spanish cattle traders or migrant workers. Although the knives were popular, the small companies and craftsmen that hand-fashioned them locally could not keep pace with factory-made versions, so production moved to Thiers. However, there has been a revival of interest since the latter part of the 20th century and there are now laguiole-style knives once more being made in the village where they were invented,

The Opinel is possibly one of the most famous knife brand names in the world. All Opinel knives bear the heraldic "Crowned Hand"

symbol of the town of St. Jean-de-Maurienne, stamped on the blade and handle. This inexpensive, folding clasp knife was invented in 1890 by blacksmith Joseph Opinel. It is a simple knife consisting of a yataghan-style blade, a pin hinge and an ash (or pear) wood handle. In addition it can have a simple steel bolster or a bolster with a locking ring – there are no springs, catches, détentes, buttons or levers… and it works every time. No wonder it became so popular with French agricultural workers. Blades can now be either the original carbon steel or more modern stainless steel. Opinels are good, all-round utility knives, and cheap enough to be easily replaced if lost. There are thirteen different blade lengths available in all, going up to a huge 225mm (just under 9 inches), with the No. 8 (85mm/3.35in) probably the best compromise for a useful pocket knife.

The nontron knife from the village of the same name in the Dordogne region are similar in design to the Opinel, but with a pokerwork-decorated boxwood handle, sage leaf shape forged steel blade and copper twist ring lock.

There are many other interesting knives available in France, but one worthy of particular mention is the so-called "vendetta" knife from Corsica, supposedly made for the local bandits to wreak revenge on each other for any slight on their honor. Antique examples are found from time to time, but modern versions are also available from companies such as Fontenille Pataud of Thiers.

ITALY

Maniago, situated in the foothills of the Alps, is one of the most important cutlery centers in Italy. There have been knifemakers there since medieval times. The local craftsman and cutlery companies are now part of a co-operative, and they market their products together. Among them are Lion Steel, Viper and Maserin. They produce some of the finest knives in Italy, both traditional and modern; in fact, they even make knives on contract for American companies.

The village of Pattada, on the island of Sardinia, is another old knifemaking center, and it has given its name to one of the most elegant of Italian knives. The pattada is a folding knife with a narrow myrtle leaf shaped blade and is still made locally, as well as in other locations in Italy.

The Italians take their knives very seriously and they produce some of the finest custom-made knives in the world. There are also many different regional knives available from companies such as Conaz Coltellerie.

COLTELLO D'AMORE – THE KNIFE OF LOVE

The Italian coltello d'amore or love knife was exchanged between a couple when they became engaged to be married. Apparently this was a custom in several areas of Italy. The exchanged knives were intended to give the man courage and confidence, while keeping his future bride faithful and safe. The handles of these highly decorated knives were normally of black buffalo horn decorated with "eyes" to watch over the owners and ward off evil spirits. Once the couple were married the knives were hung over the couple's bed.

There were similar customs in Finland, where a proposing man would give a knife to his loved one, and when married it was stuck into the wall above the marriage bed to ensure a good night's sleep… and in England a pair of knives, known as wedding knives, were given as gifts from bridegrooms to their brides.

Above: An Italian coltello d'amore, with engraved blade and highly decorated handle, made by Conaz Coltellerie.

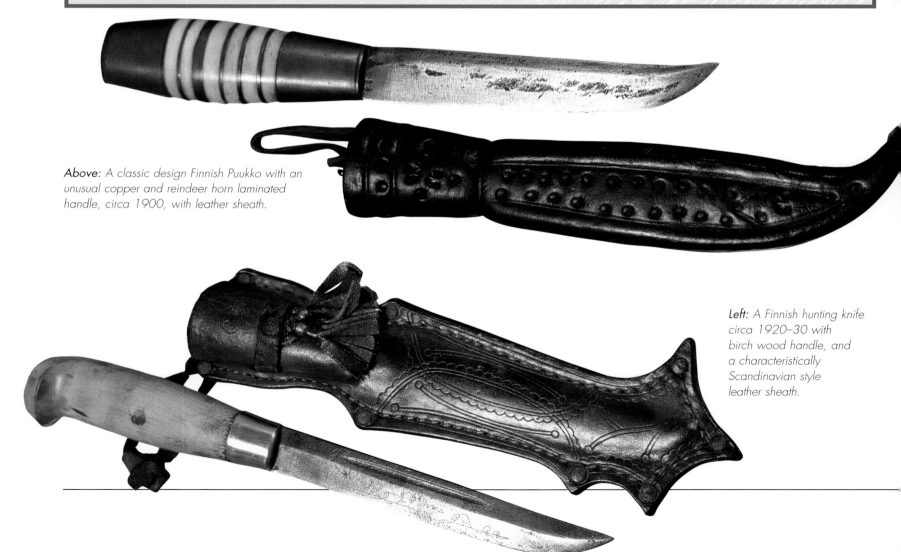

Above: A classic design Finnish Puukko with an unusual copper and reindeer horn laminated handle, circa 1900, with leather sheath.

Left: A Finnish hunting knife circa 1920–30 with birch wood handle, and a characteristically Scandinavian style leather sheath.

SCANDINAVIA

Knifemaking has always been an important industry in the Norse countries, and antique Scandinavian knives such as the leuku (or stuorranniibi), tollekniv and staskniv are highly sought after.

In Finland the traditional knife is the puukko, a simple, fixed blade, utility type often with a birch or sometimes leather-covered handle. It has a history reckoned to be over a thousand years old. Originally made for woodworking, it is now used mainly for hunting and fishing. Together with the traditional leather "tuupi" or sheath,

it is part of the customary ethnic dress of the Finns. One of the most famous makers of puukkos are Iisakki Co. who have been in business since 1879, and were awarded the title Imperial Knifemakers by the last Russian Czar.

The Tollekniv is a traditional Norwegian whittling knife, and those hand-made by Helle, a traditional knifemaker, are famous for their laminated steel blades – a forged hard steel core sandwiched between two outer layers of softer stainless steel. This gives a razor-edged blade with great strength and easy-sharpening qualities.

Brusletto, a Norwegian company has a huge range of traditional

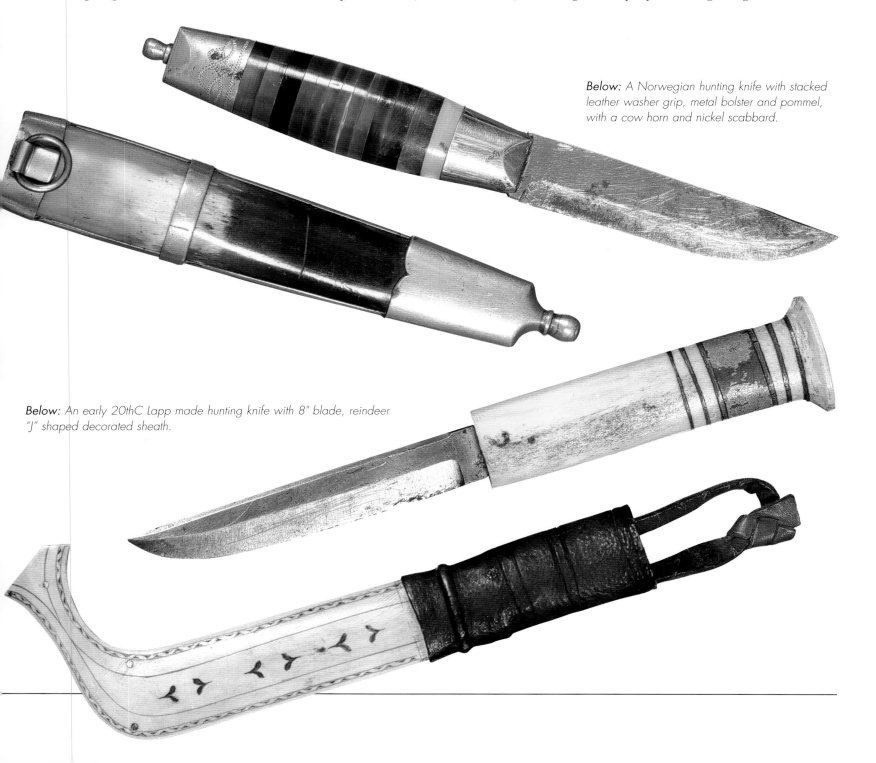

Below: A Norwegian hunting knife with stacked leather washer grip, metal bolster and pommel, with a cow horn and nickel scabbard.

Below: An early 20thC Lapp made hunting knife with 8" blade, reindeer "J" shaped decorated sheath.

Scandinavian knives, some of which can be purchased in kits or as individual components for hand assembly and finishing by the owner.

The sloyd is a popular Swedish knife, being a small, fixed blade knife with a barrel-shaped handle, giving rise to the common name of the unusual folding version – the barrel knife. Sweden is famous for the quality of its steel, and for many years it had a large and thriving cutlery industry, much of which was based around the town of Eskilstuna. The only surviving knifemaking company in the region today is EKA, famous for penknives, especially "lobster" style knives, but which also makes excellent fixed blade hunting knives, such as the Nordic range.

RUSSIA

The traditional knife of Russia is the khindjal, a version of the Arabic khanjar. It can range from the plain to the exotic, and the kama, the traditional Cossack knife, is simply another type.

Modern Russian knives can also be of exceptional quality, and innovative and artistic designs from the Basko company have won prizes for the last several years at the International Knife Exhibition at Nuremberg.

Below: A straight bladed decorated Caucasian style khindjal (or kinjal) and scabbard, as found throughout Russia for centuries – and still being made to this day. Curved blade examples can also be found.

Below: This magnificent handmade Russian "Bear" knife from Basko is unique – no two models are ever made exactly the same. Unsurprisingly the first example of this knife to be shown at the International Knife Exhibition a few years ago won the top prize.

Left and Below: Two 19thC gaucho (Argentine or Uruguayan cowboy) punales knives with silver "cutlery" style handles, embossed silver plate scabbards with some gold decoration and a "shoe" at the tip – this is usually called a "drag" on a sword scabbard.

Below: Four Spanish navaja knives, typical of the type, with narrow clip or scimitar blade and a ring pull exterior spring lock.

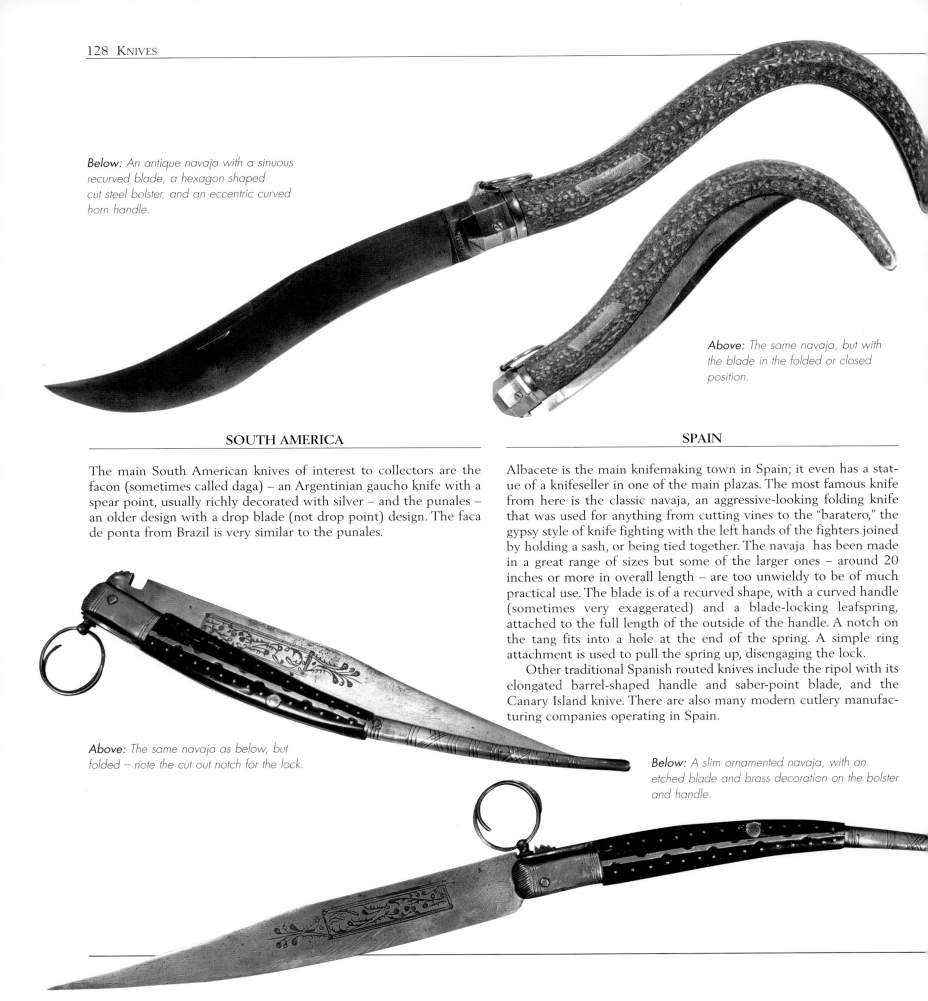

Below: An antique navaja with a sinuous recurved blade, a hexagon shaped cut steel bolster, and an eccentric curved horn handle.

Above: The same navaja, but with the blade in the folded or closed position.

SOUTH AMERICA

The main South American knives of interest to collectors are the facon (sometimes called daga) – an Argentinian gaucho knife with a spear point, usually richly decorated with silver – and the punales – an older design with a drop blade (not drop point) design. The faca de ponta from Brazil is very similar to the punales.

Above: The same navaja as below, but folded – note the cut out notch for the lock.

SPAIN

Albacete is the main knifemaking town in Spain; it even has a statue of a knifeseller in one of the main plazas. The most famous knife from here is the classic navaja, an aggressive-looking folding knife that was used for anything from cutting vines to the "baratero," the gypsy style of knife fighting with the left hands of the fighters joined by holding a sash, or being tied together. The navaja has been made in a great range of sizes but some of the larger ones – around 20 inches or more in overall length – are too unwieldy to be of much practical use. The blade is of a recurved shape, with a curved handle (sometimes very exaggerated) and a blade-locking leafspring, attached to the full length of the outside of the handle. A notch on the tang fits into a hole at the end of the spring. A simple ring attachment is used to pull the spring up, disengaging the lock.

Other traditional Spanish routed knives include the ripol with its elongated barrel-shaped handle and saber-point blade, and the Canary Island knife. There are also many modern cutlery manufacturing companies operating in Spain.

Below: A slim ornamented navaja, with an etched blade and brass decoration on the bolster and handle.

PENNY FOR A KNIFE

A custom in England requires a small copper coin to be offered as a symbolic payment when a knife is given as a gift. This custom is to prevent the bond of friendship being cut between giver and receiver. Apparently the same custom is observed in France, Spain and other countries in Europe.

FANTASY AND FICTION

A new type of blade collecting has sprung up over the last few years – the collecting of "fantasy" knives and swords associated with TV programs, movies and role-playing games. Current favorites are "edged" weapons from the films in the *Lord of the Rings* series, issued by United Cutlery. This company also distributes mythical and magical role-playing weapons designed by Kit Rae.

Most of these "fantasy" knives have unsharpened edges and are strictly for display purposes. Custom knifemaker Gil Hibben also makes some weird and wonderful fantasy designs as part of an annual series, but his exotic, multi-bladed knives have some of their edges beveled – so be warned!

Below: Gil Hibben is one of the best custom designers around for practical knives, and he can also turn his hand to fantasy daggers, such as this creation – the elaborate Eye of Drakonus dagger on its dramatic display plinth.

Left: Fantasy edged weapons are becoming big business – especially those connected with TV programs or the movies. This is a Kit Rae designed Serpent dagger mounted on a display board.

Other Applications

During the English Civil War (the struggle during the middle years of the 17th century) the infantry was split into two distinct sections – the pikemen for close work and the musketeers for long range. Once the musketeers had discharged their weapons they would be helpless in the face of attacks from opposing pikemen or cavalry during the lengthy reloading process. So their own pikemen would use their pikes – long spear-like weapons with a spike on the end – en masse to protect the musketeers. It was almost inevitable that some way of combining the two weapons would be devised, making the infantrymen more flexible, more self-contained, yet being able to support each other in both long range and close combat. The answer, eventually, proved simple – a removable blade was attached to the end of the musket, turning it into what was effectively a "short" pike. This innovation was to change battle tactics for years to come.

The name bayonet comes from the blademaking district of Bayonne, France, and the first type was a "plug bayonet." This was basically a long dagger with a round tapered handle that – at an officer's command – was wedged into the barrel of the discharged musket. This turned the musket into a close range weapon, but it obviously could not be loaded or discharged until the plug bayonet was removed.

The next development was a socket bayonet, which appeared in the late 17th century. It was a long spike or blade with a locking ring on the end, which was slipped over the barrel's muzzle. This meant that the musket could still be fired with the bayonet attached – but as the muskets were still mainly muzzleloaders, it was difficult but not impossible to reload these weapons, since the bayonets were

Right and below: Some late 19thC British Army bayonets; (top to bottom) the knife-like P1888 bayonet of the Lee Metford rifle, a Yatagan style sword bayonet (these were made for various British service rifles including some Enfield percussion carbines, Whitworths and Martini-Henrys), and the last British socket bayonet, a P1876 for a Martini-Henry rifle.

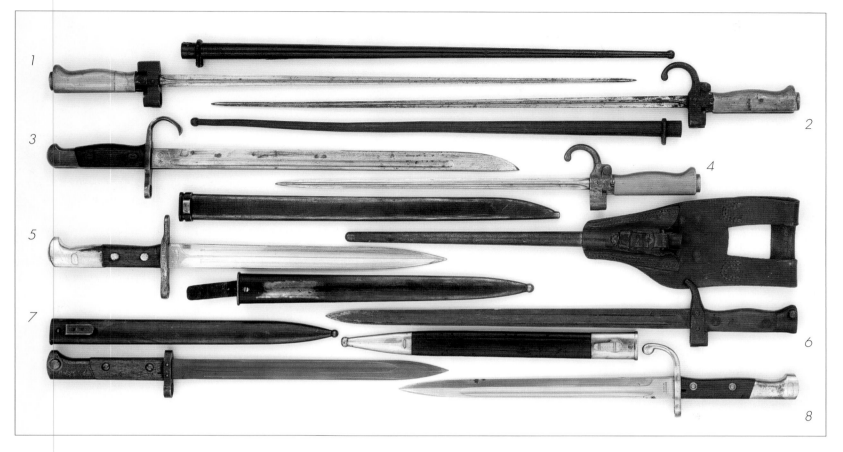

slightly offset from the socket on a short arm.

Variations of the socket bayonet continued to be used in some countries right up to the Second World War, but the bayonet blades changed considerably over this two hundred and fifty year period – from three-edged spikes through to hilted short swords which extended the length of the rifle by two feet or more. An example of this was the British Pattern 1800 Baker Sword bayonet for the Baker rifle issued to the Corps of Riflemen – made famous recently in the *Sharpe* books and TV series. This new rifle had a new kind of bayonet, more like a sword with a 24 inch blade, and it also had a new method of attachment – a mortise slot in the handle of the bayonet that located onto a bar on the barrel and was locked by a button-operated spring catch. This method of mounting became as widespread as the socket mount, and the two ran in parallel for 150 years, until the mortise eventually became the most widespread and

Above: Examples of bayonets; 1. French Lebel Mod.1886/93/16 (introduced in 1916 for the 1886 Lebel rifle). 2. French Lebel bayonet Mod.1886/1935 the final version. 3. Japanese 30th Year Type (1897 Pattern) Arisaka bayonet. 4. French Lebel bayonet Mod.1886 – the original type. 5. Swiss Schmidt-Rubin Mod.1931 bayonet and scabbard. 6. French bayonet Mod.1892 for use with the Mannlicher Berthier musketoon 1892. 7. WWII Czechoslovakian Mauser Mod.33/40 bayonet and scabbard, 8. German made Mod.1908 bayonet for the Brazilian Mauser with sheath.

is still used today. The fashion for sword bayonets caught on with armies all around the world, and are typified by the Turkish-inspired "yataghan" S-curve sword bayonet in the mid-19th century

By the end of that century the shorter, more practical knife-type bayonets had begun to be adopted, first in Germany (1871/84 pattern) and the USA (M1861 "Dahlgren"). With the advent of

Right: (top) cruciform and (bottom) round section spike bayonets for the Second World War British Lee Enfield No.4 Mark 1 rifle. A clip point knife blade with the same muzzle attachment but with no handle was also made for the No.4 rifle.

Above: The spear point American M7 bayonet – the beginnings of the combined utility knife and bayonet – with an M8 scabbard that has a self sharpening feature.

breechloading magazine-fed rifles and machine guns, the bayonet became less important. Even so, the British SMLE rifle in the First World War was fitted with a long-bladed bayonet, as was the American M1905 and the German Mauser, while both the French and Russians used long spiked bayonets (the latter being a socket type). During and immediately after the Second World War most countries were using dual-purpose knife bayonets, yet the British had just an 8in spike or a clip point blade without a handle!

In contrast, since before the Second World War, American bayonets have been very practical, with the postwar M5, M6 and M7 being as useful as a general-purpose knife off the rifle. The M9 has

continued this tradition, being adopted by US forces and the Australian Army as a bayonet, while proving popular as a utility tool and field knife with civilians. The M9 has a saw back and a slot near its clip point tip that mates to a fitting on the sheath to form an effective wire cutter. Other modern bayonets all seem to follow this utility type pattern, doubling as a general tool and combat knife – even the current British bayonet for the SA80 firearm seems to have fallen in line.

MACHETES AND SPECIAL PURPOSE TOOLS

Sometimes in military, expedition or survival circumstances, something heavier than a camp knife is required – for removing vegetation, cutting wood, building a shelter or even heavy-duty field butchery. The machete is the traditional tool for this kind of work,

Below: The US M9 is a typical modern bayonet, with features that allow it to double as a utility knife, which is why some civilians choose to purchase it for use as a survival knife and general outdoor tool.

and can be found in every corner of the world where there is a jungle. Apart from being a very effective tool, it can also be used to horrific effect as a weapon, as proved in the massacre of approximately 800,000 Tutsis by rival Hutus in Rwanda in 1994, much of which was done with machetes and similar edged weapons.

Ralph Martindale & Co. of Sheffield, England, make a 16in machete with an upswept blade called the Panga, after the short African-style machete. They also make the No.2 Golok, a standard British Army jungle issue tool, like a medium-length machete with a slimmer blade and a noticeable "wrist" a couple of inches in front of the handle. It is a very effective chopping and cutting tool, but will lose its edge fairly quickly, so it is supplied with a sharpening file in its sheath.

Cold Steel make a number of special purpose heavy blades in their Special Projects series, including modern versions of a kukri, a tomahawk and even a battle axe (or the Bad Axe as they call it). Ontario Knife Co. make a survival machete with a standard large machete, a straight-bladed machete with a saw back, a Philippine-style bolo and a cutlass-style machete designed by Blackie Collins. South American machetes usually have carbon steel blades in lengths up to 24in and handles of hardwood, rubber or plastic materials.

One of the best designs that I've seen is the Lofty Wiseman Survival Tool, a kukri-type machete, named after a famous former survival instructor with the British SAS who developed the tool with designer Ivan Williams. This, like the Martindale Golok mentioned above, is one of those tools that just feels right as soon as you pick it up.

Many of these tools are surprisingly inexpensive, and well worth considering if you do a lot of heavy-duty chopping work – it is better than working an expensive camp knife to the limit.

Left: This Lofty Wiseman Survival Tool draws a lot of its inspiration from the all purpose fighting and working knife of the Ghurkas – the kukri.

Far Left: The machete is an absolutely indispensable tool for any jungle or bush area of the world – this particular Martindale machete has a 16" blade, but some other models, especially those seen in South and Central America, can be much longer.

Left: This British Army issue machete is based on a Javanese golok jungle knife, but the narrow waist on the blade is also a characteristic of the Malaysian parang and the Philippine bolo, although they both have pointed tips rather than the enlarged "sheep's foot" profile of the golok.

Maintenance and Carrying Systems

ALL KNIVES will need to be sharpened from time to time, and, just like any other tool, the more a knife is used, the more it will need to be maintained to be kept at its optimum state of efficiency. The statement that a dull knife is a dangerous knife may sound corny but it's true. A dull knife can accidentally slip out of the cut because too much force is having to be used, while a sharp knife will require less physical effort, less pressure on the blade to achieve the cutting task, and it will give you more control. However, it is amazing how many knives are damaged, or never reach their full working potential, as the result of incompetent sharpening attempts.

THE ART OF KNIFE SHARPENING

Some people would have you believe that you need to attain some kind of higher state of consciousness before you can sharpen a knife properly. This probably comes from the East, based on the superb edges that are achieved by the Japanese with water-stones. But the plain truth is that there is nothing mystic about keeping a knife sharp – certainly not to the usable degree that most of us wish to attain.

Sharpening is all about getting the correct angle on the blade's edge – other factors come into it, such as edge thickness and smoothness, but if you can get your angles right, then you are halfway there.

The edge angle, measured from the bevel to the center of the

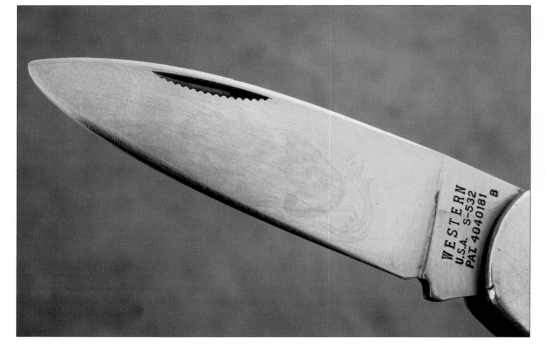

Above: This 20 year old folder has seen a lot of hard use in its life, mainly cutting ropes, and the original shape of the blade has changed with constant sharpening – a cougar etched on it has almost disappeared with wear – but make no mistake, it can still hold a wickedly sharp edge.

Below: Skinners, kitchen and butcher's knives – such as this professional skinning knife from J.Adams – need a sharp edge, so they usually have a bevel angle of about 20° (40° in all).

Below: Apart from a razor blade, the filleting knife is probably the sharpest everyday tool that most of us will use, so this often has a bevel of just 15° (30° in all), which will give a very keen edge.

bevel, so what we call a 20 degree angle is actually a 40 degree angle when the 20 degree bevel on the other side of the blade is taken into account. This is why chisel ground edges appear so sharp, because the grind is only on one side, so a 25 degree edge is added to a 0 degree unsharpened side of the blade, giving a total of 25 degrees. That is effectively sharper than a filleting knife sharpened to 15 degrees on both bevels, giving a total of 30 degrees!

WORKING WITH THE SYSTEM

Most people will just try to follow the angle that the knife came with when new, and this is certainly a sensible place to start, and the best way for beginners to achieve a consistent and correct angle is to use a commercial sharpening system. As a colleague of mine recently said, "Keeping a knife sharp by hand is one of those things that you either can or can't do, and for all of those who can't there are sharpening systems."

With a sharpening system, such as those made by Lansky, Gatco

blade, can vary considerably, depending on the task for which the knife is specifically designed – the tighter the angle, the sharper the blade should be. Although an edge angle can be as acute as 10 degrees on a scarily sharp razor, you will normally find that 15 degrees is the tightest you will come across, and that will give a very sharp edge to filleting knives and the like. Generally speaking, an angle of about 20 degrees is used on kitchen knives and skinners, 22 to 25 degrees for hunting and pocket knives, 25 to 28 degrees for more robust hunting and utility use, and 30 degrees for a long-lasting edge on a heavy-duty camp knife. Above this – 32 to 40 degrees – and you are talking about the kind of edge found on chopping tools.

When talking about edge angle we are referring to only one

Below: The American style tanto, introduced by Emerson, is an excellent design, and as the chisel grind is beveled only on one side it can be kept extremely sharp. This model is the CQC7B folder with a half plain, half serrated, ATS34 steel blade.

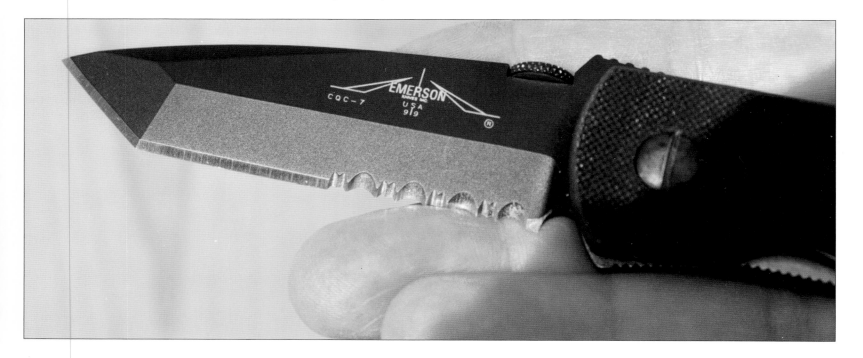

Above: *This pedestal mount is a handy accessory for the Lansky sharpening system, and leaves both hands free to hold the knife and the stone's plastic handle. This picture shows the stone, guide rod and blade clamp in use – note the different edge angle slots on the clamp.*

Left: *This is the standard three stone Lansky sharpening system, but it can be augmented with extra stones, holders, etc.*

and DMT, you can control the angle of the edge bevel by using the pre-set angle holes in the system's guide clamp. I use a Lansky system, but all of them work around much the same idea. Lansky's basic kit consists of a set of three hones (fine, medium and coarse) set into color-coded plastic holders, guide rods, honing oil, a T-shaped selectable angle guide clamp (with four angle settings – 17, 20, 25 and 30 degrees) and a carrying case. I also use an additional ultra-fine hone, a medium "diamond" hone and a V-shaped ceramic hone for serrated blades. Each hone comes with a thumbscrew to fit an L-shaped guide rod.

To use the system you just secure the spine of the knife in the angle guide, then select the hone – usually coarse or medium to start with. You fit a guide rod to the hone, and slot it into one of the angle holes in the guide, corresponding with the type of edge required on the blade. A drop of sharpening oil is applied to the face of the hone, which is then laid on the horizontal blade. Then you work in a series of push/pull motions, with light pressure being applied on the forward stroke only – you let the hone do the work. The holder can be easily reversed so that both sides of the blade can be honed without removing the knife from the guide. As the knife gets sharper you change down to finer stones until you reach the degree of sharpness that you require.

While the system works well, you still have to hold the guide in

one hand while moving the selected stone with the other. The job is far easier if the holder is fixed, leaving you with both hands free to operate the stone. There are three mounts available for the Lansky system – a pedestal, a universal mount and a Super C Clamp. The pedestal is a simple plastic mount that can be screwed to any flat work surface – ideal for a permanent fixture to a workbench. The Universal is made of alloy and is a simple table mount. But in my opinion, for mobility and versatility, the alloy Super C Clamp is the best bet. This two-part C type clamp can be quickly fixed to most horizontal and vertical board-type surfaces without the need for screws.

FIELD USE

For touching up a knife edge in the field a small portable sharpener is preferable to a sharpening system, for obvious reasons. A small natural stone, a diamond hone, ceramic "sticks" or a mini-butcher's steel can all be used. The original Arkansas stones are excellent for putting a good edge on a carbon steel knife, and a steel can be very effective if an aggressive edge is required (although it may become dull more quickly). For some of the tougher modern steels a manufactured abrasive stone using ceramic (aluminum oxide) or a diamond type sharpener is a more effective choice.

Above: *While a small Arkansas stone is still one of the most popular for field use, more knife users are switching to portable commercial systems, like Eze Lap diamond hones or the illustrated Gatco Tri-Steps combination plain and serrated edge sharpener .*

FREEHAND SHARPENING

This subject is worth a book on its own – and that's just what I would recommend. *The Razor Edge Book of Sharpening* by John Juranitch, first published in 1985, is virtually the industry standard. Don't feel that you have to follow it slavishly, but it certainly contains all the fundamentals of sharpening and will give you a far deeper knowledge of the subject than I can impart here.

CARRYING SYSTEMS

Fixed blade knives for outdoor use come with a sheath of some kind, usually made to be carried on a belt. For instance, most hunting knives and the like are supplied in a traditional leather sheath. If looked after, these will give years of service and are inexpensive to repair or replace.

Below: *This MOD (Masters Of Defense) CQD folding knife has three carrying systems, a formed leather sheath, a Cordura pouch that can be attached to a rigid plastic frame and a rigid plastic scabbard that allows the knife to be carried in the open position – like a fixed blade.*

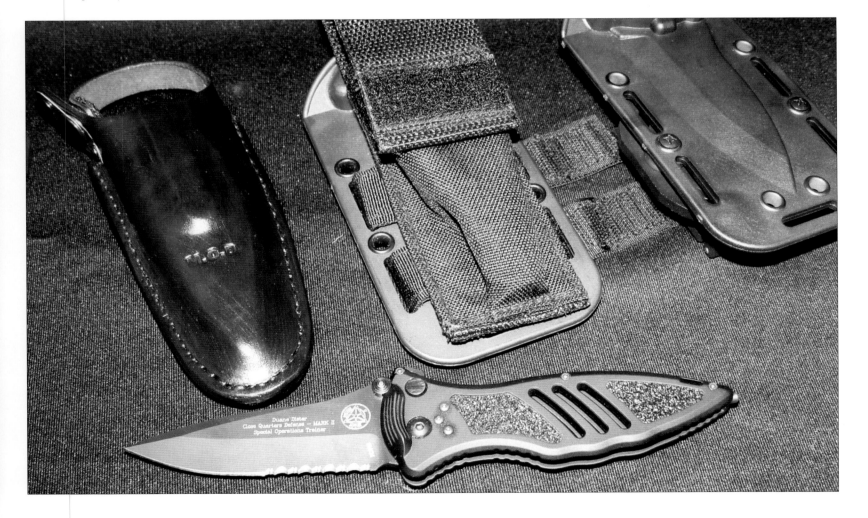

Ten Rules of Knife Use and Maintenance

1. Always keep your knife sharp. It may sound surprising, but more accidents occur when people try to compensate for a blunt knife by exerting more cutting pressure on the cut, then slipping or losing control of the blade.

2. Never hand a knife to another person "blade first." If it's a folder, then fold it before passing it over. If it's a fixed blade, hold the spine with the edge facing away from your hand and offer the handle.

3. Take time and care when sharpening your knife – many knives get damaged by owners rushing the job or not following the instructions that come with the sharpening system.

4. More often than not the weakest part of a knife is its tip, so never use it as a pry-bar or screwdriver unless in an emergency. If you really feel that you can't do without a pocket pry-bar in your day to day tasks, then buy a chisel point rescue or diver's knife that's made for the job.

5. Keep your knife as clean as possible – including the handle, not just the blade. Three of the most common corrosives that knives come into contact with are salt, sweat and blood. So clean your knife as soon as practicable after each use, especially if it has been used for skinning and dressing game or fish, or been in the vicinity of acidic or alkaline substances. Knives can usually be cleaned with a damp cloth, then buffed off with a clean, soft, dry cloth. If necessary wash them with a mild liquid detergent first, then rinse off and dry. Always wipe off and wash blades before food preparation.

6. Do not leave your knife immersed in water, or exposed to excessive heat or sunlight. Each of these conditions can lead to either discoloration or bleaching, there's also the possibility of organic material like wooden hand grips warping, and adhesives can breakdown.

7. Never throw a knife that you can't do without – because you can damage the tip even if thrown correctly and damage the whole knife if thrown incorrectly… you can also lose it altogether. If you really want to throw knives as a sport, then either buy those that are designed for the purpose or adapt knives that you already own and keep them just for throwing.

8. Do not put oil on leather sheaths, since it can discolor the leather and sometimes breaks down the stitching. Instead, use saddle soap to clean, and dubbing (a type of water-resistant shoe wax) to protect the leather.

9. Keep blades protected during temporary storage with a light coating of wax. Metal bolsters and most handle materials can be treated with wax in the same way. High carbon blades or just the exposed edges of powder-coated blades can be given a light coating of petroleum jelly for protection.

10. For long term storage put the knife and sheath (separately) into a sealable plastic bag, preferably along with a sachet of Napier's VP90 or a similar vapor-type protector, but if this is not available, then a good quality desiccant can be used at a pinch.

Some modern knives – including military models – may be supplied with sheaths made from canvas or synthetic fabric (such as Cordura or Kydex) or even rigid plastic. Some designs can be quite complex, such as the multi-positional sheath (featuring a rigid polymer Tek-Lok belt fastener) by Blade-Tech Industries as supplied with the Camillus CQB, or the very professional multi-carry rig made by tactical webbing specialists Black Hawk, supplied with CRK's Green Beret. These types of rig offer options of carrying on a standard waist belt (vertically or horizontalyl) or on your webbing, or they can be strapped to upper or lower leg or even your arm, although the last two are not that practical. They can also be used in the "opposite" shoulder (left if you are right-handed), in the handle hanging down position. While this rig is often seen in the movies, a serving soldier with lots of urban fighting experience told me that it can prove awkward if you have to fire your rifle from the opposite shoulder, such as when firing around a corner.

Some civilian knives also have versatile carrying systems, such as the Bud Nealy MCS, which can be used to carry a knife in at least half-a-dozen different ways, but be sure to find out if your state or country legislation permits concealed carrying of a fixed blade knife.

With folding knives there are three options for carrying – a belt pouch of leather or synthetic material, an integral belt clip on the knife, or just loose in your pocket! The latter option is OK for slip-joint knives, but not so good for locking knives, since grit, dust or fluff from the bottom of your pocket can get into the mechanism and cause it to fail if the lock doesn't engage properly and you don't notice the fact. Belt pouches are fine, and will keep the knife clean and secure, but they can be bulky and in some cases difficult to open with one hand. I prefer the integral belt or pocket clip, mainly for its ease of access. The problem with a clip is that if you are climbing

Below: A versatile Blade-Tech Industries rigid scabbard with a shaped gripping throat and a multi-positional Tek-Lok belt fastener – this type of carrying system is becoming more popular in both military and civilian applications.

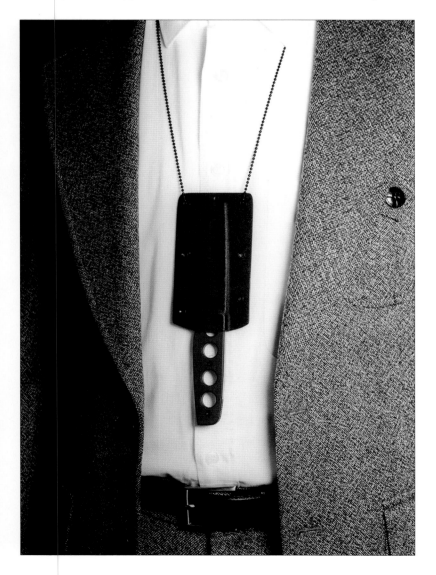

Below: The Bud Nealy MCS (Multi Carry System) knife by Boker is designed to fit belt, waistband, pocket or boot and is seen here in the neck carry mode.

around and the knife snags up, it can be pulled off its anchoring point and lost. Attaching a lanyard acts as an insurance policy, but also gives you something else to snag up! A good compromise is to clip the knife to the inside edge of your pocket where it is unlikely to snag but is kept away from the grunge that always seems to accumulate in the depths of your pocket.

As you can see, each method has its pros and cons, so just pick the one that suits your particular needs best.

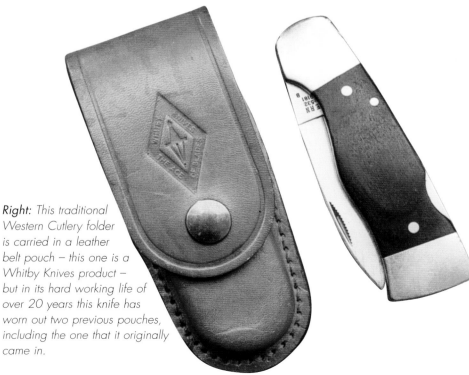

Right: This traditional Western Cutlery folder is carried in a leather belt pouch – this one is a Whitby Knives product – but in its hard working life of over 20 years this knife has worn out two previous pouches, including the one that it originally came in.

Glossary of Terms

ABS: An impact-resistant plastic sometimes used for handles and sheaths.

African blackwood: A very dark mahogany, almost black, with tight graining, used for custom knife handles.

Alumina ceramic: A hard man-made abrasive used for sharpening.

Annealing: The process of heating and cooling steel slowly to make it "workable" for shaping and grinding. Different methods, temperatures, heating and cooling times are used to achieve particular results.

Antler: The horns of deer (which are shed annually), a traditional material for knife handles.

Arkansas stone: A type of naturally occurring rock, cut into rectangular blocks and used for sharpening.

Arkansas Toothpick: Dating from the mid-19th century in the USA – any large, heavy, self-defense dagger with a needle pointed blade.

Arm knife: A knife–which could be in one of many different shapes and sizes–carried on the upper arm by some North African tribesmen.

Back lock, rocker bar lock or lock-back: A lock that uses a spring and rocker bar with a pawl, in conjunction with a notch on the tang, to lock the blade of a folding knife in the open position.

Bail or shackle: A metal ring on the end of a knife for attaching it to a ring clip.

Ballistic cloth: A heavy nylon-type material, such as Dupont Cordura, used for personal military and outdoor sporting cargo carriers, such as webbing, sheaths and knife pouches.

Barlow: A Sheffield folding knife design with a long bolster – for extra strength.

Barong: A long Philippine leaf-shaped knife used by Moro tribesmen.

Bayonet: A blade or spike that attaches to the end of the barrel of a military rifle.

Bead blasted: A matt or satin abraded metal finish achieved by bombarding with tiny glass beads.

Black oxide: A black coating, especially for non-stainless steel, that stops reflection and improves corrosion resistance.

Bolo: A large machete-type knife from the Philippines.

Bolster: A supporting or reinforcing metal piece at the blade end of a knife handle (especially on folding knives but sometimes also on forged steel fixed blade knives).

Bowie knife: A large knife, epitomized by a long heavy clip point blade, made famous by American frontiersman James Bowie in the 19th century.

Butt cap (or pommel): A supporting or reinforcing piece at the end of a knife handle, usually made of metal.

Camp knife: A large knife that can also be used for chopping.

Canoe: A twin-bladed pocket knife with a canoe-shaped handle that curves up at both ends.

Caper: A skinning knife for more delicate tasks like removing the mask from a skull.

Carbon: The mineral that is added to iron ore to form steel.

Carbon fiber: An exceptionally strong and lightweight man-made sheet material consisting of woven graphite fibers bonded in epoxy resin. Sometimes used for knife handles and scabbards.

Choil: The word may come from the Celtic word for "thin" but it now means a semi-circular cut-away area in front of the guard of some knives; it may be large enough to fit a finger, or just a tiny cut-out area.

Clip point blade: A blade on which a "clip" is taken out at the tip end of the blade's spine, giving a finer and lower set point.

Cordura: See Ballistic cloth

Cross-guard: See Guard

Crucifom: A slim cross-section blade, usually for reinforcing a needle point for stabbing weapons as found on some old daggers and bayonets.

Cryogenic quenching: A modern method of quenching tool steels by using extremely low temperature media.

Cutlery steel: Any steel which is suitable for making knives.

Dagger: Normally a spear point or saber point blade; can also be a narrow stiletto-type knife.

Damascus: A composite, pattern-welded steel made from two or more different steel types.

Desert ironwood: A dense-grained wood from the Sonoran desert in northern Mexico, used for top grade knife handles.

Dirk: A single- or double-edged dagger or any hunting or defensive knife with a long slender blade.

Dropped edge: Where the bottom (edged) part of the blade is deep just in front of the handle so that the hand cannot slip forward – as seen on many classic chef's knives and also some gaucho knives.

Drop point: A popular blade design where a shallow curve drops a little lower than the spine to meet the rising sharpened edge, resulting in a slightly lower tip (a drop point).

Edge grind: The angle and design of the bevel that is ground away to form the knife blade's edge.

False edge: A sharpened bevel (angle) on the spine of the blade, as sometimes seen on a clip point. A decorative unsharpened bevel (also seen on some clip point blades) is called a swedge or swaged edge.

Flint: A type of hard stone used to make the first knives.

File work: Decorative patterns filed into the metal of a knife, usually on the blade's spine or frame edge.

Fleam: A special blade used for the medical treatment of livestock.

Fuller: A groove along the center of the blade flat to lighten and stiffen it, sometimes wrongly called a "blood channel" or "blood let."

G-10: A lightweight woven glass fiber for knife handles that is strong and easy to grip.

Guard (also cross-guard): A metal plate, with or without one or two extended arms (quillons), separating the blade from handle to stop the user's hand slipping onto the blade edge.

Haft: Another name for a handle or grip.

Hardening: Heating steel to its critical temperature (austenizing), then quenching (fast cooling – unlike when annealing) to harden. Different quenching mediums – oil, water, air, etc. – are used for different types of steel.

Horn: Domestic cattle or black buffalo horn used for some traditional knife handles.

Interframe: The metal inner "chassis" of a folding knife, usually with grip scales of a different material to form the handle.

Jeweling: This is a round machined, abraded pattern used in the shotgun trade for reflecting light in attractive patterns from the metal surfaces of an opened action, and is now being used on the internal liners of some custom folding knives.

Jigged bone: Bone handle carved to look like antler.

Kraton: A man-made rubbery plastic material ideal for knife handles.

Kydex: A tough plastic used in the manufacture of sheaths.

Linerlock: A blade lock on a folding knife, formed by a sprung section of the liner that blocks the tang, preventing accidental closure.

Micarta: Linen, canvas or paper bonded in an epoxy resin to form a strong, tough material for knife handles.

Niello: A black, metallic, powdered alloy used to fill engraved designs on the surface of metal, sometimes used on ancient and antique dirk handles, ricassos and scabbards.

Quillon: A protective metal "arm" that protrudes from the knife's guard.

Ricasso: A small, unbeveled area on the blade between the guard and the edge.

Scales (also grip scales): The two halves of a handle.

Slip-joint: A non-locking mechanism that holds a folding knife's blade in place, open or shut

Tang: The unsharpened portion of a fixed blade knife to which the handle or grip scales are attached.

Tempering: A lower heating and cooling process used after the hardening process to stop warping and distortion caused by internal stress.

Steel: A combination of iron and other elements from which most blades are made.

Zytel: An impact-resistant, lightweight plastic used for grips.

Index